MONTANA Madams

By Nann Parrett

FARCOUNTRY
PRESS

Dedication

I dedicate this book to my husband, Dr. Aaron Parrett, for putting his eyeballs over countless drafts, for constantly talking me off the ledge, and for having confidence in my ability to see this daunting project to the end. I also dedicate it to my sweet daughter, Maizy P, who always has a smile, a hug, and a joke for me when I need it most. Thanks for your patience throughout this whole process, little one. I'm all yours now, sweetpea.

ISBN: 978-1-56037-634-7

© 2016 by Farcountry Press
Text © 2016 by Nann Parrett

For more information about our books, write Farcountry Press, P.O. Box 5630, Helena, MT 59604; call (800) 821-3874; or visit www.farcountrypress.com.

Library of Congress Cataloging-In-Publication data on file.

 Produced and printed in the United States of America.

20 19 18 17 16   1 2 3 4 5

Table of Contents

Chapter 6: The Madams of Miles City and Billings—
Untamed Women on an Untamed River

Chapter 7: Bozeman—*A Hotbed of Vice*

Acknowledgments

When I first took on this project, I had no idea of what I was getting myself into. I walked into the office of Ellen Baumler, Helena's expert on Montana madams, and told her I was to write a book on the history of Montana madams. Her response? "That's an ambitious project . . . what's your timeline?" Six months, I told her.

"Wow. Good luck with that."

More than a year later, I can't believe this manuscript is actually going to print, and it still feels grossly incomplete. The stories of the elusive women in this book had me tearing at my hair again and again. Just when I thought I had nailed down a personality, I would find conflicting information that countered everything I thought to be true—oftentimes right at deadline.

I am no historian. I fell into this project when I was hitting up Farcountry Press for some editing work, and Will Harmon asked me what I thought about writing a book. I didn't think about writing a book. It never occurred to me that I would ever *want* to write a book. Let alone a history book. But I am one who enjoys scaring myself on occasion, so I took the bait.

I have thoroughly enjoyed the process of doing the research required for writing this text. I obsessed on compiling stacks and stacks of information, sifting through the clues, and developing conclusions about what these women's lives must have been like. I would like to thank the actual professionals who helped me make some sense of it all.

First and foremost, Will Harmon has been an incredible editor to work under, and I really appreciate his insights, humor, and words of encouragement. I feel fortunate to have had the opportunity to work with him. Never once did he shame me for not making a deadline. (One time I told him I would eat my shoes if I missed a date, and he bounced back a picture of loafers made out of freshly baked bread.)

To the staff of the Montana Historical Society's research library, I am indebted for all of their assistance in leading me down new rabbit holes and subsequently pulling me back out. I would like to especially thank Ellen Baumler for fact-checking and providing feedback for the Helena section of my manuscript. As well, I would like to thank individuals from the various regions whose fact-checking and expertise were crucial throughout this process—Mary Gleim expert Kim Kaufman, Virginia City historian Leona Stredwick, Fort Benton and Great Falls historian Ken Robison, Powell County Museum and Arts Foundation curator Melanie Sanchez, Great Falls history reenactor Alise Herodes and the Downtown Chicks, Billings historian Kevin Kooistra of the Western Heritage Center, and Bozeman's Dia Johnson.

Perhaps the most interesting part of my research was interviewing individuals who had contact, directly or indirectly, with women I wrote about. Susan Bazaar, Norman and Harry Barnett, and Sidney Armstrong showed me a very personal side of Ida Levy; Lee Harrison (daughter of Justice John Harrison) and city planner Pete Lenmark helped shed new light on Big Dorothy.

Now that this book is completed, I feel a huge weight has lifted . . . but I'm already feeling the hint of a new weight bearing down on me. It would be a disservice to those I've written about—as well as those I've opted to omit from this particular text—if I were to simply walk away without another thought. Stories are buried, and people need to take the time to pick through the archives and piecemeal these stories together to bring these women back to life. We owe it to them.

At first glance, the impulse of any amateur, armchair historian is to level judgment upon these characters. But doing so reflects a one-dimensional view of the historic record. We have to work through our knee-jerk sentiments and get past them, because these women are complex. They had to be, given their circumstances. They were scared. Brave. Quiet. Opinionated. Smart as all get-out. Lacked judgment. Often Inebriated. Keenly clear-headed. Euphoric. Distraught. Likeable. Detestable. Whimsical. Sincere. Trusting. Skeptical. Trustworthy. Deceitful. Lusty. Reserved. Silent. Rambunctious. Tired. Indefatigable.

They are, in a word, people like everyone else, and therefore reflections of who we are as individuals. As such, they are sympathetic characters about whom we ought to want to learn more, because they are reflections of who we might have been under similar circumstances.

On top of that, it will take any researcher a lot of conscientious legwork to get past the offhand, hyperbolic remarks of territory journalists as preserved in microfiched newspapers to really capture the essence of these formidable women who helped shape our culture, and to get past sugar-coated accounts that covered the tracks of individuals wanting to preserve their legacies before we can draw solid conclusions about these elusive women.

Can we love these women *and* detest them? The profession they chose demands such ambivalence.

I say yes. We can do both.

Mothers of Vice
Making a House a Home

The oldest adage in economics might very well be that "prostitu-tion is the world's oldest profession." In a casual way, the propo-sition is certainly true. The world's most ancient work of literature, for example, *The Epic of Gilgamesh* (circa 2500 BCE) features the "harlot" Shamhat—an interesting first appearance, since in that narrative it falls to Shamhat to "civilize" the hero by introducing him to love. The Bible abounds with references to harlots and concu-bines, and there, too, prostitutes play a significant role in many of the best-known stories: Samson and Delilah, Mary Magdalene, the woman at the well, and so forth. One could draw the historical con-clusion that, for better or for worse, prostitution is closely associated with the dawn of civilization, which is of course another way of say-ing that "prostitution is the world's oldest profession."

This book, however, is about Montana "madams" in particular, which immediately raises two questions: what is the relationship be-tween prostitution and being a madam, and what, specifically, did that mean in the history of Montana? We can address the first question quite easily. In a nutshell, a madam managed the careers of prostitutes. It's interesting that a madam might therefore be conceived as the female equivalent of a pimp, but through the course of this book I hope to show that such a transposition would be unfair and ill-advised for a variety of reasons. One of these might be made clear by analogy: while men may make excellent and expert gynecologists, one thing they cannot bring to the profession is experience of what it means to inhabit a female body. For whatever else they were, madams were not pimps, at least not in the sense of the word as it is used today in ordinary conversation.

Surely, many madams came into their occupation in the way you'd expect. They were originally prostitutes who, for one reason or another, left that working class to join the managerial class, much the way that some clerks work their way up to become CEOs. Others, however, made a more lateral transition into the field: perhaps they started out managing a hotel or saloon and simply diversified their offerings. Or perhaps a woman whose husband died in the mines suddenly found herself without the wherewithal to support a family and so turned her home into a boarding house, which segued into a house of ill repute. Perhaps they watched their male counterparts fattening their wallets by managing sex operations and jumped into the market knowing they could do it better by running their business more efficiently and, quite possibly, more humanely. It was a more psychological game for the madam.

Pimps provided management, but they differed from madams both in theory and practice. To a pimp, a prostitute was merely property on loan, a commodity to be peddled over a card game or a shot of whiskey, a deal to be closed with a handshake or a slap on the back. For a madam, on the other hand, a prostitute was an employee who represented the house where she was working and most likely residing. While the pimp would serve as an agent of street traffic, the madam would operate from and provide at least the semblance of domestic stability. You could not have a madam without a "house."

A successful madam understood the psychology of her employees, clients, and community. She knew how to gain the trust of those individuals who could potentially help her and, to keep herself in the favor of those who might readily shut down her operation, applied best practices and marketing techniques. She used her common sense, balancing her experience as a mother with a keen business know-how with her ability to bat her eyes and drop a punchline, winning the hearts of those around her. She could even, on occasion, throw a left hook to get her point across.

It so happens that Montana, in contrast to the rest of the country, came to civilization relatively recently and almost entirely under the scrutiny of recorded history, which provides us a unique opportunity to observe the role of the madam from the very beginning right up to the 1980s when the last practicing madam in the state closed her doors. Accordingly, the history of madams operating in Montana offers an intriguing entry into the local history of various communities. Exploring the lives of these madams provides us an opportunity to observe the social climate of earlier eras and to consider the factors—economic, industrial, and sociological—that affected the trade and, in turn, helped shape the local community.

The stories here are organized by region, beginning with the first towns that sprung up from the initial gold strikes in the Montana territory, since these places lured the initial wave of women seeking their own fortunes: Bannack, Virginia City, and Alder Gulch. Next I discuss the Helena region, then move on to Butte and Anaconda. From there we travel to Great Falls, then to south-central Montana and the agricultural and railroad towns of Miles City, Billings, and, finally, Bozeman. These are a handful of the better-known locales throughout Montana. It goes without saying that prostitution operated in virtually every nook and cranny of the state. I have overlooked more rural madams in favor of their urban counterparts because the available research resources diminish in direct proportion to a business's distance from an urban hub.

Because staid historians invariably viewed prostitution as a shameful or detrimental aspect of community development, and because women throughout history have been viewed as second-class citizens, the historical record itself is scant and often frustratingly terse on the topic. Only recently have thorough studies of prostitution been made available, the best known of which emphasize the appearance and practice of prostitution in the larger cities, such as Chicago *(Sin in the Second City: Madams, Ministers, Playboys and the Battle for America's Soul* by Karen Abbott), for example, and New York *(City of Eros: New York City, Prostitution, and the Commercialization of Sex, 1790-1920* by Timothy Gilfoyle). But there have also been excellent contributions to the history of prostitution in the West as well: Michael Rutter's *Upstairs Girls: Prostitution in the American West* and Jeremy Agnew's *Brides of the Multitude: Prostitution in the Old West,* both preceded by Anne Seagraves' *Soiled Doves: Prostitution in the Early West.*

Thanks to the proliferation of women scholars and an increasing public interest in cataloging the lives of figures previously relegated to history's margins, and renewed interest in the social roles of madams as well as their economic function in the West, studies such as *Frontier Madam: The Life of Dell Burke, Lady of Lusk* by June Willson Read, *Minneapolis Madams* by Penny Petersen, and Lael Morgan's *Wanton West: Madams, Money, Murder, and the Wild Women of Montana's Frontier* are available. Local authors have also documented the history of Montana women of the night, including Paula Petrik and her book *No Step Backward* as well as local historian Ellen Baumler and her many written contributions.

Acknowledging my great debt to the more scholarly works that are available, I have taken a casual approach in the hope of personalizing the lives of these women and preserving their often vibrant and charismatic characters in a book for readers who perhaps share a love for the shadier side of the Old West. And while madams are probably not the most suitable icons of feminism, they provided throughout history one of the few opportunities for women to operate their own businesses and succeed in establishing economic security. They often did so by exhibiting the political acumen and social skills necessary for negotiating with city fathers and their clerical counterparts. At the same time, the curse of prostitution was a touchstone for early feminists who first gained momentum as part of the temperance movement of the mid-nineteenth century. This movement recognized both alcohol and prostitution as the two leading contributors to the oppression of women.

Because madams operated as a matter of course in tension with the more respectable elements of the community, they tended to be women of unusual character—intelligent and witty, often shrewd and ruthless in business, and perceptive and politic. Some of the madams in Montana enjoyed, at least on a local level, something of legendary status, and in this book I bring stories alive for readers in a way that I hope will encourage them to appreciate the compelling complexities of the lives of these women and their often neglected contributions to the fabric of Montana's social history.

Pioneering Petticoats
The Madams of Bannack and Virginia City

In 1862, gold fever struck Montana. A few prospectors had seen promising colors as early as 1858, but in late July 1862, all hell broke loose on Grasshopper Creek, a tributary of the Beaverhead River, when John White discovered a bonanza. Within weeks, a camp sprang up, and not long after, a second strike was made along Alder Creek, some eighty miles to the northeast. Within months of the strike on Grasshopper Creek, saloon keepers and prostitutes who had a shrewd sense for supply and demand in the western mining camps began to arrive. In less than a year, both sites had become booming communities—Bannack and Virginia City—with all the standard institutions of any Wild West boomtown: saloons and pool halls, hurdy-gurdy houses, and hotels with dance halls.

Once a saloon or dance hall opened its doors to the public, the owner printed tickets and sold them for fifty cents or a dollar, entitling the purchaser to a drink and dance token. A prospector would then spend the token on a dance with the woman of his choice,

The town of Bannack sprung up around the placer diggings on Grasshopper Creek and by 1864, shown here, boasted bakeries, hotels, a jail, bowling alley, saloons, and brothels.
PHOTOGRAPH COURTESY OF THE MONTANA HISTORICAL SOCIETY RESEARCH CENTER, 940-696.

which created an opportunity to bargain for further services if the woman was so inclined. There was no shortage of work in the sex trade for early female arrivals. When it became the territorial capital in 1865, Virginia City's population reached 5,000, but, according to one old-timer, only twenty or so were women, "and most of them were trollops."

Women often slid into prostitution by way of a dance hall or saloon that featured "hurdy-gurdy girls," a slippery term that does not unequivocally refer to a prostitute, although in practice it often could. Hurdy-gurdy girls were hired to be present and available for "dancing" in the saloons, although the literature is often unclear about what precisely "dancing" entailed. Early accounts give the sense that writers were perhaps uncomfortable spelling out the details and so settled on the euphemism of "dancing." In any case, if "dancing is merely the vertical expression of a horizontal desire" (variously attributed to George Bernard Shaw, Oscar Wilde, and Robert Frost), it's easy to imagine how a customer's expectations might not gibe with that of his dancing partner. Some women danced as entertainers, scantily clad or topless, further blurring the picture. In any case, the distinction between a saloon and a dance hall was mainly a matter of emphasis: a saloon featured drinking and offered dancing, while a dance hall featured dancing and offered alcohol.

Dance hall girls were not prostitutes in the ostensive meaning of the term, but they did often find themselves pursuing work outside the terms of their hiring, and so were often held in contempt by women who had crossed the line and were offering their services openly as prostitutes. Hurdy-gurdy girls, on the other hand, were advertised as "dancing girls," but were also known to take money for sex at their own discretion. One can see why antipathy might arise between the two classes of women.

Like so many aspects of the West, Hollywood has perpetuated a largely false image of the typical dancing girl in the early boomtowns. In the movies, the dance hall girls inevitably appear in trios around a piano, with operatic voices, lulling the drunken cowboys or miners with sweet melodies. In reality, the music in the earliest establishments would have been provided by crude string bands featuring fiddles or guitars, or perhaps a banjo or a concertina, since pianos were extremely difficult to transport to the frontier. Moreover, the women of such places were also economic opportunists rather than musical hobbyists, and they would be much less likely to lure in customers with their discordant melodies than they would be to circulate out in the crowd, drumming up a dance or further business. That business would have been conducted in rooms built above the saloon or dance hall.

Brothels were also an important part of mining community economies in the West, and in early Montana they operated openly and with community consent. Eventually, when communities became more settled and politically organized, madams and prostitutes paid fees to the city or to law enforcement for licenses to conduct their business.

Unfortunately, the historical record remains woefully limited as to the specific identities of the territory's earliest madams. It's true that almost every document that records day-to-day life in Bannack or Virginia City refers frequently to the prevalence of alcohol, gambling, and prostitution, but few of them go into much detail. According to a pamphlet distributed by the Montana Historical Society, these

Business buildings lined both sides of Virginia City's main street in 1866.
PHOTOGRAPH COURTESY OF THE LIBRARY OF CONGRESS, HABSMONT, 29-VIRG, 2-1.

early-day prostitutes would have been indistinguishable from "respectable" women while in public, probably only by the lack of a wedding ring. Decency laws mandated that women cover their ankles, and prostitutes most definitely would not have openly strolled around in their corsets and petticoats—the equivalent to today's bras and underwear. According to living-history interpreter Leona Stredwick, Virginia City's jezebels were likely the best-dressed women in town. Like many women they wanted to feel pretty, and they had money and ready access to the finest ladies garments available.

Two trade routes ran through Virginia City. Boats traveling the Missouri River delivered commodities to donkey trains, which then carried the goods along a treacherous route from Fort Benton through Mullan Pass west of present-day Helena. Most of the payloads came from the South, where Virginia City was sending a lot of gold to support the Confederate cause. The other trade route came from San Francisco by way of Salt Lake City. This brought more Eastern goods, such as fine silks from China and exotic fruits from South America. A person could get anything for a price, and many scarlet women enjoyed the fineries usually only afforded to ladies of high society. Parlor ladies were known to eat meals of wild bird and choice-cut beef served on ironstone and fine porcelain while drinking wine from crystal goblets. Such conspicuous consumption conveyed to clients and other members of their community that they, essentially, had arrived. These were women with refined taste, who demanded some level of respect.

According to Stredwick, "...if a miner offended a lady of the evening, there were ten miners ready to take him out because a lady is a lady."

Prostitution houses were often run like the company stores that operated at mines or other large-scale industrial enterprises. The prostitutes were expected to purchase their clothing and other necessities under their madam's account at a local store, for example, with the madam then extracting a measure of interest on the purchase. Madams generally required their girls to purchase their own dresses, the quality of which again depended on the quality of the house where they were employed. Women working in "cribs" or shabby bordellos invariably settled on simple cotton dresses that provided uncomplicated access, whereas women working in classier establishments dressed in fine silks cut in the latest fashions.

While the many scholarly books on prostitution discuss the social customs and nomenclature associated with the subject, Linda R. Wommack's *Our Ladies of the Tenderloin: Colorado's Legends in Lace* provides an excellent overview of how such businesses tended to be handled in the West in the nineteenth and early twentieth centuries. The author explains that like any service industry, from the perspective of the practitioner, the quality of the workplace could differ dramatically. A brothel, for example, was a step below a "parlor house." While both might be overseen by a madam, the brothel provided services at a rate often far below that of a parlor house, which often translated into a noticeable difference in the quality of clientele. Similarly, parlor house girls were held to higher standards of dress and social conduct than were their brothel counterparts.

Hygiene was a critical issue. In the days before local and state health department oversight, managing disease was left up to the women themselves, under the watchful eyes of their madams. In a way, hygiene was self-regulating and directly connected to the quality of the house, since the prevalence of medical complaints was the central factor in an establishment's reputation. What did hygiene consist of in practice? For starters, in the higher-quality parlor houses, women were required to change the linens between customers; they were expected to thoroughly wash themselves between customers; and perhaps most beneficial, they took it upon themselves to discreetly scrutinize clients before attending to the task at hand.

In contrast to the proprietors of parlor houses, madams who ran brothels tended to be less circumspect in choosing the women they hired, willing to employ those who were less attractive or perhaps past their prime. This of course translated directly into a difference in cost that then winnowed the wealthier customers from the poorer ones. At the same time, a brothel offered its workers much less freedom of movement and less choice in working hours than did the parlor house. Even worse for the women working in the brothel, madams there generally extracted a higher percentage from their earnings.

Another feature of the prostitution economy bears comparison to the company store economy. Instead of operating on a purely cash basis, many houses and brothels used tokens—brass coins specific to an establishment—so that madams could better keep accounts, with less ambiguous customer transactions. A customer who bought a brass coin or token was entitled to a specific liaison with a woman, for example. In this way, cash was exchanged for "house money," much in the way that gamblers even today must purchase house chips to sit at a casino's poker table. At the end of the business "day," the madams inventoried the coins to balance the books.

May Wilson, a Miles City madam, issued tokens that clients used to pay for services. According to the 1904 City Directory, Wilson resided at 115 Pleasant Alley, where she ran a "female boarding house." PHOTOGRAPH COURTESY OF THE TOKEN STORE.

As one would expect, the volume of traffic tended to be higher in a brothel than in a parlor house, simply because of the lower cost. This meant that in practice brothel girls worked harder and longer than their counterparts at a parlor house in order to make the same wage. To draw an obvious analogy, a fast food worker at McDonalds earning $8 per hour must put in considerably more hours at an arguably more demanding job than her counterpart at a high-end restaurant who draws $24 per hour in tips.

Madame Moustache— A Rambler and A Gambler

The Cosmopolitan was a dingy, two-story gaming house and brothel on Front Street in Fort Benton. It was sandwiched between Dena's Jungle and the Phoenix Bar, part of a long string of Front Street venues—Mose Solomon's Medicine Lodge, the C-King Foon, The Occident, and the Board of Trade to name a few—that catered to the throngs of rowdy characters congregating there. Fort Benton was a bustling trading post at the eastern end of the Mullan Road, a 624-mile wagon trail connecting the Rocky Mountains to the Inland Northwest. The road served as a transportation corridor for transferring cargo from the steamboats landing at the topmost navigable point on the Missouri River to those waiting on the Columbia at the other end, which would then continue to carry the loads to the Pacific Coast and the various points between. In its initial years, the Mullan Road saw considerable traffic. After its completion in 1862, it was estimated that as many as 20,000 travelers made the trek along stretches of the road, as well as 6,000 horses pulling wagon loads of goods and some 5,000 head of cattle. A good portion of these travelers steered toward the West Coast to settle, likely crossing paths with those who thought better of it and were returning home. Other folks regularly traversed back and forth, transporting supplies to peddle throughout the region at phenomenal markup, while others followed the Mullan Road to seek quick fortunes in surrounding boomtowns, journeying between Helena, Bannack, and Blackfoot City. A handful of others took the route to find fresh victims to swindle, or to escape from the places they'd been and the people they knew. Entrepreneurs,

Eleanor Dumont's gambling house and brothel in Fort Benton, the Cosmopolitan, stood in the middle of what was known as "the bloodiest block in the West," which occupied today's 1500 block near the walking bridge. PHOTOGRAPH COURTESY OF THE MONTANA HISTORICAL SOCIETY RESEARCH CENTER, 947-075.

trappers, outlaws, prospectors, whores—a good many of them sought opportunity in the new frontier via the Mullan Road and likely passed through Fort Benton at one time or another.

A fair amount of blood spilled on that infamous Front Street stretch, known as "the bloodiest block in the West." Over pilfered wallets, lost lovers, underhanded aces, or old vendettas—rarely a day went by without a good scuffle, shootout, or knife fight. The Front Street brothels, bars, and gambling dens butted up against each other, facing out toward the banks of the Missouri River like an indomitable line of seasoned showgirls waiting arm-in-arm for their male habitués to come sauntering in off the steamboats.

A person entering the Cosmopolitan could drink, gamble, and cavort with loose women around the clock. One time, an itinerant steamboat man with $200 in his pocket, Louise Rosché, stopped in "for a fling at cards" with the "lady boss." Inside, it reeked of smoke, sweat, and cheap whiskey. A ramshackle bar lined one wall, and men stooped around various gambling tables, laying their money

Eleanor Dumont, aka Madame Moustache, made her name on her charm and cunning at the card table. PHOTOGRAPH COURTESY OF THE FRED MAZZULLA PHOTOGRAPH COLLECTION (SCAN # 10035412), HISTORY COLORADO.

down for rounds of cards or dice, while one lone table sat empty on a raised platform in the middle of the room—reserved for Eleanor Dumont, the notorious madam in charge.

She always welcomed unwary fresh faces to her table with her warm smile and lilting, singsong voice: "You will play, M'sieur?"

From upstairs Rosché could hear "the click of dice, the rattle of the roulette ball, and the slap of cards." He took a seat at the bar and handed some money to a woman working there. He told her to go buy herself a drink.

"Come around after I clean out the Madame," he told her, "and maybe we can do a little celebrating." The heavily painted prostitute rolled her eyes and told him not to hold his breath. Suddenly, a hush fell over the room. A heavy-set woman wearing an ornate, black silk dress entered. It was none other than the head lady of the house. According to Rosché's account, "Rouge and powder, apparently applied only halfheartedly, failed to hide the sagging lines of her face, the pouches under her eyes, the general marks of dissipation."

She typically dealt cards for *vingt-et-un* at her table, a popular frontier game that was the French predecessor to blackjack. A plumpishly petite woman in her late thirties, she entertained her male counterparts with her deliciously French-glazed elocutions and light-humored jabs. The men were immediately drawn to the wild, dark curls piled atop her head, which were accentuated by her dazzling, black eyes—to then be countermanded by the bristly patch of whiskers sprouting from her upper lip.

Branded "Madame Moustache" just a year before, while she was living in Bannack, Dumont was unsuccessful at shaking her new nickname. Apparently, a kvetching patron had thrown down the insult after losing at her table, and the name followed the notorious card-dealing madam as she moved throughout the Rocky Mountain region, all the way to the end of her life.

Rosché didn't last long at Madame Dumont's table. She cleaned him out before he was even able to warm up his seat. She insisted he wasn't allowed to leave until he had a special drink on the house, however. Her bartender brought Rosché a glass of milk. In her gentle, congratulatory tone, she said, "Your special drink, Mr. Steamboat Man." It was a gesture she extended to all losers at her table.

Born around 1829, Eleanor Dumont was likely lured to the West by the promise of fast-won riches. She arrived in San Francisco in her early twenties, around 1850, and went by various names—Simone Jules, Emiliene Dumont, Eleanor Dumont, and Sara De Vallerie. A stunning beauty, she claimed to be the daughter of a Frenchman, Viscount De Vallerie, who lost everything during Napoleon's Reign of Terror. According to her story, she was forced into an arranged marriage with a cruel man who imprisoned her in his country chateaux for five years after she was caught trying to elope with a man from Marseilles. As the story goes, she was able to escape and eventually made her way to the Barbary Coast where she landed a job dealing cards in a gambling hall called the Bella Union. Current-day historians postulate that hers was a fantastically spun tale, with her true roots being in New Orleans, but her experience at the Bella Union did gain her regional popularity. She had refined sensibilities in an environment that was bawdy and boorish, and men swarmed to her table. Madame Moustache eventually opened up her own gambling house after losing her job at the Bella Union. (She was so good at the game that she was accused of card sharping.) Her own venue was quite successful, but she eventually felt the lure of freshly panned gold, knowing she could win it directly, fair and square, from the miners' hands. She headed to Nevada City in California, the largest and most civilized mining town behind San Francisco and Sacramento. The arrival of this small woman having "a form almost perfect and with grace of movement rarely equaled" startled even the most hardened of Nevada miners—especially when they learned of her unmatched gambling skills.

She arrived there in 1854, stepping off the train coach, glamorously dressed in the highest fashion and turning all the heads around her. San Francisco had its fair share of upscale women, but in this dusty frontier town, such a sight was astonishing. After checking into a local hotel under the name of Eleanor Dumont, she set out to walk along Broad Street, the main thoroughfare. Everyone's interest was piqued as she peered into the windows of the many empty shops. In a matter of days, the townsfolk understood her intent. She distributed a handbill inviting everyone to the grand opening of the "best gambling emporium in northern California," the Vingt-et-un. Attendees were promised a game with Madame Dumont, with free champagne to boot. Who could resist an invitation like that?

This establishment was like none other. Women, other than the one in charge, were not allowed to enter or loiter out front. Despite this, the venue had an air of sophistication. With plush carpets underfoot and gas chandeliers overhead, men were required to be well groomed and well behaved if they wanted to play at Madame Dumont's Vingt-et-un. Swearing was not allowed. Having such a beautiful, quick-witted woman running the place was a novelty, and miners did not shy away from its high standards of good behavior. Men continued to groom themselves and flock to her table, even when on a losing streak, because her presence was irresistible—and because she had gained the reputation for playing an honest game. If a man made any advances, she kept him at a distance while calmly rolling her cigarettes. Whenever the sport at the card table grew heated, she coolly applied her silver tongue to soothe her hot-tempered guests. She once even used her mediating skills to intercept an angry mob of unemployed miners and Mexican laborers, preventing a major riot.

Business was so good that Miss Dumont entered into a partnership with fellow gambling ace David Tobin, and opened Dumont's Palace, offering vingt-et-un, faro, keno, roulette, and poker. An orchestra played under the gas lights, and the Palace was a raging success, making the owners very wealthy. According to historian John G. Lepley, the partnership blossomed into a love interest, until Tobin demanded more than fifty percent of the earnings. Dumont refused, so they closed shop and parted ways.

Eventually, the gold of Nevada City dried up, so Dumont headed over to the next burgeoning town of Columbia. And from there on, to Silver City and Salmon, Idaho, Corinne, Utah, and wherever else new gold strikes beckoned. Eventually, she landed in Carson City, Nevada, where she set her mind to leaving the gambling business and settling down in a quiet town. She bought a ranch, knowing very little about raising livestock. She met a handsome man who claimed to be a cattleman. Some accounts say he was the dashing Jack McKnight who had a gambling house where Madame Dumont headed a table. Other accounts say he was a cattle buyer named Cai Carruthers. Whatever the case, she married a man and figured he would know how to keep a ranch afloat. Madame Dumont handed him the responsibilities of managing the place, signing over all of her property to her husband. Within one short month, however, his true colors were revealed. He sold the ranch and skipped town with everything, leaving Dumont destitute and outraged. She had never been one to let a man get close to her. When she did let down her barriers, she got nothing but grief. It was a hard lesson to learn, but she was not one to sit back quietly and be defeated.

According to several accounts, from that point forward, she packed heat with her wherever she went, on the offhand chance she might cross paths with her two-faced former companion. A few years later, McKnight was found shot full of holes. Reports claim Dumont was suspected, but there was never enough evidence to convict her of the crime. One account states that the sheriff following the case never pressed her too hard for information, knowing full well the hell she had gone through with that man. Legend has it that, years later, Dumont confessed to the crime.

The years that passed were not gentle on Madame Dumont. Something happened to her as she drifted from one town to the next. Over time, she bore little resemblance to her former self. In the beginning, she had been enticingly aloof, distancing herself from her leering, roughnecked patrons. They placed her on a pedestal, where with poise and grace she courteously rebuffed their advances and reminded them that she was a respectable woman with refined manners. But each new town left its mark, and she developed the callouses to prove it. One Chicago reporter noted, "She had a once-handsome face which crime had hardened into an expression of cruelty. Her eyes glittered like those of a rattlesnake and she raked in the gold dust or chips with hands whose long white fingers sharp at the ends reminded me of a harpy's talons." After she opened her first brothel in Bannack around 1864, the hardness of her life began to show its effects. Her elegant gambling houses gradually morphed into seedy whorehouses with worn gaming tables. Her words more often echoed the crass language of her associates. The dignified lady who could once pacify a couple of desperados itching for a fight transformed into a gun-toting battle-ax, meeting any transgressor eyeball to eyeball, causing them to cower and scurry away.

One account tells of her heading home on an exceptionally successful night of gambling, only to be accosted by two men who demanded that she hand over her winnings. She shot one man dead, while the other fled. Another time, while she was living in Fort Benton, word went around that a steamboat was heading toward town with smallpox victims aboard. Dumont met the boat at the levee, waving a pistol in each hand. She threatened she would shoot the pilot full of holes if he dared to dock. Needless to say, the boat spun around and headed back downstream. She reportedly marched back into the Cosmopolitan and ordered drinks for everyone on the house, becoming the overnight town hero. Her venue quickly became the most popular hangout on Front Street.

Madame Dumont's notoriety shifted from that of an incredibly gorgeous and refined lady of the felt to being a force to be reckoned with, yet an honest force. Her staid reputation for dealing an honest game kept her customers coming back. She always paid the winners in full, with a gracious smile, and she always made good on her debts.

Around 1868, Madame Dumont uprooted again and headed north, to the Kootenai Mines in British Columbia, where word had it one could find "gold dust like cucumber seeds." She was one of the first to arrive in the area and sank all of her spare cash into hiring some contractors to erect a gambling saloon and dance hall. The rush to the area proved uneventful, as the area's riches fell far short of expectations. She headed back south to Montana, still owing money to the contractors she had hired in Canada. Madame Dumont landed in the boomtown of Blackfoot City, home of the largest Montana gold nugget discovery. She quickly recovered her losses and was flush with cash when she moved to Elk Creek and eventually Reynolds City. She learned that the contractors to whom she was still indebted were working in that town. To their pleasant surprise, she tracked them down and paid the full amount she owed in bankable gold dust.

Madame Dumont continued to follow the call of gold, winding her way through Nevada, South Dakota, and eventually landing in Tombstone, Arizona. There she was reported to have dressed the women of her house in the finest of clothes to then parade them up and down the street in a resplendent carriage, all the while puffing away at her cigar.

By the time 1878 rolled around, Madame Dumont was living in Bodie, California, where she would spend her final days. After living there for about a year, she found herself running her table with a low bank, so she borrowed $300 from a friend to keep the game going. Within a few hours, however, she had completely run out of funds, handed over the keys of her establishment to her creditor, and walked out. The next day, Madame Dumont was found about a mile away, some distance off the road, lying on the ground with a rock for a pillow. She died from drinking wine laced with morphine and left a letter leaving directions for what to do with her estate, along with a statement that she was "tired of life."

MADAM HALL'S GRIEF
AMONG "THE INNOCENTS"

Bannack's black sky was devoid of a moon on the icy night of January 10, 1864. The sub-zero air crystalized every exhaled breath of the spectators encircling a recently constructed scaffold. In the center of the ring stood the town sheriff, Henry Plummer, and his two deputies, Buck Stinson and Ned Ray, all three accused of belonging to a secret society called "The Innocents." The gang was presumably responsible for a series of gold thefts and murders along the main travel routes of the frontier. Above them, three nooses dangled silently, awaiting their warm necks.

The three men had been summarily rounded up by vigilantes—the Montana Vigilantes—and marched to the hanging site that night after another man, Erastus "Red" Yager, according to the Vigilantes, identified the three in an attempt to save his own throat from hanging. (He wound up in the wrong end of the noose anyway, despite the "confession" he made.) Stinson, still wearing his best Sunday suit, was dragged from the house where he was boarding with his wife. The Vigilantes had found Ned Ray garbed in buckskins and sprawled flat out on a table, passed out, in the Yankee Flats Saloon. Both men put up quite a struggle as they were escorted out; enraged and cussing, they did not go easily.

The gallows at Hangman's Gulch in Virginia City were simple but effective.
PHOTOGRAPH COURTESY OF THE MONTANA HISTORICAL SOCIETY RESEARCH CENTER,
STEREOGRAPHICAL COLLECTION.

Sheriff Plummer, on the other hand, wept, pleading for his life. He begged for one final prayer, to which one of the Vigilantes nodded upward toward the rope, "Certainly, but say your prayers up there."

Ray was hoisted first. A former engineer who had turned professional gambler, he had a reputation for cavorting with known outlaws in the region. While in Salt Lake City, Utah, he had been convicted for rustling mules, but managed to escape prison and make his way to Bannack, where, despite his roughneck reputation, he was never known to have another run-in with the law. In fact, Sheriff Plummer appointed him as a deputy to work on the right side of the law. As he was dragged toward the rope, Ray struggled and spewed profanities at his captors, who slipped the first noose around his neck. They raised him a few feet, then dropped the cord. In a last, desperate attempt to prolong his life, Ray reached up to grab the noose as he fell. That one maneuver was enough to prevent his neck from breaking, so he did, in fact, prolong his life—for a few silent and agonizing minutes. The circle of onlookers watched as he thrashed about at the end of his tether. In *A Decent Orderly Lynching—The Montana Vigilantes*, Frederick Allen described the lurid scene. "[H]e dangled in the frigid night air, strangling, his contorted face illuminated by torchlight and his desperate gasps for breath silencing all other sounds. It took him several minutes to die."

As Ray swung there, the other two men were brought to the center of the ring. After watching his comrade silently struggle, Plummer pleaded for a "good drop." He and Stinson were subsequently raised to the greatest height their ropes could afford. When they dropped, their necks instantly broke. Although Ray was the first to hang, he was the last to die.

In the distance, a woman's distressed wailing distracted the spectators. It was Ray's lover, Madam Hall, owner of the saloon and dance hall up on Yankee Flats on the south side of town. One account described her cries as "making the night hideous." She raced toward the gallows when she heard that her lover was slated to be strung up that night. A small party of men went to greet her before she arrived at the hanging site.

"Where is my Ned?" she demanded.

"Well, if you must know," responded one man, "he is hung."

Just as her lover had bitterly and profanely objected to that night's necktie party, so did Madam Hall as she flung a long string of forceful insults and obscenities at the men who roughly shoved her away from the hanging site and escorted her to her cabin nearby. Various accounts noted that her piercing wails kept the townsfolk awake throughout the night. Meanwhile, the three men's bodies were left to dangle and sway through the frozen hours until dawn.

Friends of the three men returned to the hanging site the next morning to cut down the corpses from their ropes. Stinson, Ray, and Plummer were carried to town and laid out in a row, shoulder-to-shoulder, on the floor of a makeshift morgue in an unfinished log cabin. Madam Hall arrived to transfer her lover's corpse to her home, where she prepared it for burial herself. Stinson's wife also showed up, though less out of love than avarice: she came to retrieve her husband's wedding band, and when she found herself unable to pull it from his stiffened finger, she simply cut off the finger in order to get the ring. Plummer's wife—a woman of good social standing and probably wholly unaware of any of her husband's illicit shenanigans—never showed to bid a final farewell to her husband.

Although Madam Hall was allowed to dress her lover for a proper burial, Ray and the other two men were buried in shallow, unmarked graves near the hanging site. Sheriff Plummer's body was the only one encased in a wooden coffin.

MATTIE LEE— TWO MEN FOR BREAKFAST

The silver mining town of Granite sits in the brushy foothills of the Flint Creek Range, about three miles east of Philipsburg. There, at about three in the morning on March 30, 1891, Mattie Lee burst into Sam Green's saloon with a man at her heels in hot pursuit. He lunged forward and grabbed her, and the two started struggling and arguing while about ten patrons paused mid-sentence over their drinks to watch. What had led to their public squabble? A feisty round of the card game known as "casino."

The excitable man, Jack McDonald, was a stranger to town, a ticket taker at Butte's premier variety and burlesque theater called the Comique, who had come to visit a sick friend. That afternoon, he had dropped by Mattie's "house" for some entertainment and a few rounds at the poker table when things went afoul on the felt. He tried his hand at casino, an old Italian card game that was especially popular in nineteenth-century America. It was fast-paced, usually two people playing head-to-head, with the object of the game being the first to collect twenty-one points by winning tricks containing aces, the two of spades, or the ten of diamonds. Like other popular games of the era, such as gin or whist, casino mixed skill with luck. Players usually played for a dollar a point, and the points could add up quickly. McDonald was betting a dollar a point for each game, holding his cards gingerly because he had banged up his hands rather badly in a barroom brawl the night before.

Mattie Lee ran houses in Fort Benton, Elkhorn, Butte, Granite, and Virginia City. She spent time in the penitentiary for killing a man, after which she disappeared from the public record. PHOTOGRAPH COURTESY OF THE POWELL COUNTY MUSEUM & ARTS FOUNDATION.

Consequently, he was in a bit of a mood, annoyed because of his sore hand but perhaps also because he kept missing sweeps and getting stuck with tough hands for three rounds running at the table. He was down by three bucks. With his pockets nearly empty, he decided to take his chances once more and tripled his bet in the fourth game to reclaim his losses. McDonald won, relieved to have escaped a tromping, and decided it was time to collect his earnings and go.

But his opponent, madam Mattie Lee, was not about to pay up. Nothing annoys a gambler more than to see a hard-earned stack of chips get pulled away after a lucky break. After a few heated words, she grabbed the stash in the pot and rushed out the door, up Main Street toward Sam Green's place, where she was sure to find some empathetic comrades to hide behind.

An angry McDonald caught up with her in the saloon, and Mattie struggled to free herself from the crushing grip of his good hand. Perhaps feeling some nostalgia for the old days of his career as a Butte town cop, McDonald announced he was going to arrest the prostitute for illegal gambling.

"I will just take you up town and see about this," he fumed, dragging Mattie down the hall, intending to take her to the sheriff as she struggled in vain to wrench herself free.

Listening in from the other side of the door, one of Mattie's friends happened to hear the set-to, a fellow named Frank McKeen. He was quite possibly Mattie's main paramour, in fact, and happened to be coming to Sam's place for an after-hours drink. He had just turned out the lights and locked up his own saloon in the same neighborhood, an establishment called the Kentucky Liquor Store. Hearing the heated exchange, McKeen burst into Sam Green's place and asked what was going on. To that, Mattie replied she was being held prisoner, a state of affairs that he could confirm with his own eyes. McKeen confronted McDonald, telling him he had no business keeping the woman, since he was not an officer of the law. Naturally, McDonald had a different opinion.

According to one newspaper account of the court trial, McKeen made several attempts to escort Mattie out the door, but McDonald slammed it shut, blocked the exit, and then grabbed the other man by the collar. He thumped McKeen on the ear and reached around his victim's torso, groping at his pockets to feel whether he had a gun or not.

McKeen did happen to be armed, carrying his prized .41 Long Colt with pearl grips, which under normal circumstances would have been left back at his own establishment, beneath the bar. But in the last few weeks, a string of burglaries there had made him apprehensive about leaving the gun unattended. McKeen grabbed the firearm before his assailant could get his hands on it. The two men tussled wildly, crashing down the entire length of the bar as they vied for possession of the pistol, and throughout the ordeal, feisty Mattie took advantage of the situation to get in her own kicks and sucker punches at the entangled out-of-towner. A customer held her back, fortunately for her, for the first shot from McKeen's gun went through the front door. McDonald continued grappling for the gun as another shot fired, this one harmlessly hitting the floor. A third slug pierced the wall. Finally, a fourth shot rang out, and McDonald dropped flat.

The bullet had pierced his thigh. McKeen made for the door, and a customer hollered after him that he couldn't leave.

"You keep back," McKeen replied. "I am going to give myself up to an officer."

If McDonald had died right then and there, Sam's place would have had "a man for breakfast" that night, as the saying went, a euphemism for a dead man on the floor.

But he wasn't dead. The local doctor was called in to assess his wound, and, not surprisingly, the prognosis was not good. Even if the doctor were to amputate the leg, McDonald's odds of survival were dismal, even for a gambling man: he had only one chance in a hundred to survive. The young man and former cop from Butte at first refused treatment, finding it hard to fathom that he was facing his own mortality on that fateful night.

But McDonald had pushed his luck too far this time. His condition rapidly spiraled downward over the next twenty-four hours. He ultimately relented to the surgery, and his leg was removed the next day, right below the hip joint.

With long odds stacked against him and stuck with a hand even worse than what he'd been dealt in his card game with Mattie Lee, McDonald died and was laid out, minus one leg, a couple days later. It turned out that Sam Green's place did have a man for breakfast after all. It just took a few days for that man to get served.

Frank McKeen went on trial for murder, and Mattie helped her friend by ante-ing up the cost of a good defense lawyer. The attorney was able to convince jurors that her friend killed Jack McDonald in self-defense.

Thanks to Mattie, McKeen walked away a free man.

Mattie Lee—also known as Mattie DaVere and Dutch Matt—had accumulated considerable wealth working houses in Fort Benton, Elkhorn, and Butte before her move to Granite. Originally a widow from Augusta, Maine, she likely fell into the hard path of prostitution because, like many other women of her era, she saw it as her only path to self-sufficiency.

During her residence in Fort Benton in 1883, the local paper described her as "a frail beauty." But, apparently, prostitution and heavy drinking quickly took a toll on her. Only seven years later, a hyperbolic *Anaconda Standard* reporter portrayed her as "[o]ne of the worst and most repulsive looking creatures of the whole army of prostitutes now living in Granite." It was probably difficult for Mattie to stomach such harsh public criticism, and she was likely most grateful when Frank McKeen, the man she helped save from prison or the gallows, returned her favor by helping her to start over in a new town 150 miles away.

McKeen bought her a brothel in Virginia City, called The Green Boarding House, located in the heart of the town's red light district and adjoining the Chinese district, right across the street from the Chinese temple. She stayed there until 1901, when she left the state. One account said she headed with her sister for Denver and another stated that she moved to Wyoming. Whatever the case, she apparently felt more at home in Montana, because she returned two years later in December to open another house in Philipsburg, where she would find herself faced with a strangely familiar scene.

One evening, a Finnish wood hauler named Charles Hillman (by some accounts, the name was Hillson) came to town from a nearby wood camp with drinking on his mind. He visited Mattie's place for the afternoon, and once inebriated, ducked out without paying his tab. Mattie, well-known as a formidable drinker herself, happened to be fairly lit, and she chased him down, finding him seated in a neighboring saloon. She demanded from him the money he owed her, but he argued he wasn't about to pay up because he didn't owe anything.

Mattie Lee's boarding house, left, was adjacent to the Green Front boarding house on the right, in the heart of Virginia City's red light district. The two smaller log structures were brothels run by Myrtle Butler and Pearl McGinnis. PHOTOGRAPH COURTESY OF THE MONTANA HISTORICAL SOCIETY RESEARCH CENTER, 956-426.

"You don't, eh?" she exclaimed. "Well dig up!" at which point she pulled out her .38 caliber Harrington & Richards and popped off a shot. The bullet ricocheted off his ankle and hit the floor.

Hillman was either in shock or even drunker than he appeared, as he looked at her deadpan, without so much as a flinch. He hardly acknowledged that she had fired a shot. She gritted her teeth like she were ready to spit nails. Raising her pistol again, she held it steady and pointed it straight to his head. For some reason, his nonchalance seemed to spur her fury even more.

Still, he didn't blink, and something inside of Mattie snapped.

The next shot she fired straight through his eye, directly into his brain, and Hillman fell to the floor in a heap—another man for breakfast.

According to an account in the local paper, Mattie remained at the scene, waiting for police officials to arrive, as she frantically explained to onlookers that Hillman had it coming. And the locals gave Mattie a sympathetic ear, because the Finn and his fellow countrymen had won themselves the reputation of being "troublesome" and "obnoxious." After her trial, everyone was surprised that she received a stiffer sentence than expected.

Mattie Lee was not as lucky as her erstwhile friend, Frank McKeen. No locals came to her defense, so she asked McKeen to help her out. Even though he secured her a notable defense lawyer who argued insanity as Mattie's reason for the shooting, she still got the full ten-year sentence at the state penitentiary in Deer Lodge for manslaughter.

Washed up and in her forties, she didn't fare well in confinement and was reportedly "broken down from drink and the nervous strain." Years of fast living and hard drinking had taken their toll, and in prison she rarely ate and soon became a physical wreck. She had lived hard, and had lived through hard times, but none of that compared to serving hard time.

Once she had served her sentence, Mattie Lee more or less vanished from the public record. The years of drinking and gambling had culminated in a grim stretch in the pen, and whatever pleasures of the flush years that remained were dim memories of boisterous parties turned sour.

Madam Mattie Lee was responsible for the serving of two men for breakfast in her time, both at prices far dearer than the few dollars they had fought over.

Origin of the Term "Red Light District"

The pejorative term "whorehouse," unprintable in nineteenth-century newspapers, often gave way to terms such as "boarding house," "gilded palace," "gilded palace of sin," "gilded palace of human weakness," "house of ill repute," "house of disrepute," "house of sin," "bawdy house," "house of assignation," or some other combination thereof. (Into the twentieth century, the pretense evolved into something more along the lines of "furnished rooms.") Not surprisingly, the houses of prostitution that most madams ran tended to be relegated to the less-than-desirable districts of town. These sections were often colorfully named with their own euphemisms: "the badlands," "the tenderloin," or "the red light district."

The neighborhoods that madams operated in were often a few blocks from the genteel main thoroughfares, but close enough in proximity to provide ready access. At the same time, those sections of town tended to be located near railroad switchyards in warehouse districts. One of the most common terms for a neighborhood in which madams plied their trade is "red light district," which various sources suggest is a reference to the red lanterns that railroad workers used. Because of the fire hazard of wooden sidewalks that were common in the day, the men were said to have hung their lanterns upon the doorways of the women whom they visited, to avoid tipping them over and causing a blaze, which led to red lanterns signifying the skin trade in general. The Oxford English Dictionary indicates that the first use of the term dates to 1894, and cites a Sandusky, Ohio, newspaper article as the first appearance in print.

The urban legend research group Snopes.com points out that, by this logic, red light district could just as easily signify a neighborhood of bars or taverns. Other plausible accounts theorize that it was the prostitutes themselves who provided the red lights in their windows as advertisement.

It may be a chicken and egg argument as to whether the railroaders or the prostitutes first used the red light terminology, but the fact that such districts were commonly in the vicinity of the railroad yards

*is probably responsible for many other terms for sketchy neighbor-
hoods, including phrases like "the wrong side of the tracks." Railroad
terminals and switchyards in the nineteenth and early twentieth
centuries generated ungodly amounts of pollution (locomotives
burned coal, and not very efficiently) and noise, so that the nic-
er parts of town naturally were located away from the tracks. At
the same time, businesses catering to the working classes who
could not afford to live away from the noise and smoke did locate
near the tracks—dive bars, greasy spoon restaurants—and houses
of ill repute.*

Helena

A City of Capital Delights

Nine weeks after a weary and defeated Robert E. Lee shook hands with Ulysses S. Grant in the parlor of the McLean house in Appomattox, Virginia, bringing the bitter American Civil War to a quiet and final end, a mysterious woman named Fannie Bird became the first woman to officially purchase under her own name a piece of property in the bustling mining camp of Last Chance Gulch, nearly 2,200 miles to the west, in a new territory of the United States called Montana. The news that Lee had finally surrendered his exhausted Army of Northern Virginia, putting an end to a violent conflict that had split the nation for four long years, traveled quickly to the rowdy little town in the heart of Montana Territory. Although the community around Last Chance Gulch, today known as Helena, may have been far removed from the skirmishes and battlefields of the Civil War, its early history was intimately entwined with the enmity between Northerners and Southerners, since a considerable number of Confederate sympathizers helped establish the town. In fact,

27

a local grade school, Four Georgians Elementary, commemorates the discovery in 1864 of gold by four displaced Southerners, or so the legend goes, and another huge strike east of Helena a few months later was christened "Confederate Gulch." By one account, even the pronunciation of the name "Helena" was subject to debate and fell along party lines. Unionists insisted it should be pronounced "HELL-uh-nuh," in imitation of the name of a town in Minnesota, whereas the Confederate sympathizers, known as "copperheads," rallied for "Huh-LEE-nuh," after a town along the Mississippi in Arkansas. The fact that this rogue town deep in the wild Montana Territory had its fair share of Southern sympathizers who were so recently disappointed and dismayed by the South's tragic flogging made Fannie Bird's purchase of some local real estate a rather interesting accomplishment and a feat worthy of mention in the history books. Not so much because she was a woman, but because she was a *black* woman.

And yet, in spite of this singular purchase of note, Fannie Bird remains almost entirely a mystery to recorded history. She's mentioned here and there, with references to her connections to prostitution and her ownership of property, but little else can be gleaned from the historical record about who she was or what kind of woman she may have been. Nevertheless, a few inferences seem reasonable. She must have possessed a brave spirit and the resolute strength of character necessary for the trip west, especially for a black woman while the country was in the throes of a war waged almost entirely on whether or not the South would be permitted to maintain its practice of enslaving black people. But the frontier afforded opportunities denied to women and black people in the East if for no other reason than the West lacked a critical mass of population to support the rules and conventions of "civilized" society with any regularity.

Many women hustled their way through the West, hoping to carve out a slice of their own from the wealth that the miners and speculators were drawing from the mountains. Mining towns came and went as prospectors hit pay dirt, mined until the lodes depleted, and moved on in search of fresh veins. With the waves of transient miners came the prostitutes vying for direct access to those men's treasure—a sort of trickle-down economics that one sees even today in western

As seen here before the August 1872 fire, downtown Helena was dense with wood-frame buildings among a scattering of brick and masonry shops and hotels.

WILLIAM HENRY JACKSON PHOTOGRAPH COURTESY OF THE U.S. GEOLOGICAL SURVEY DENVER LIBRARY PHOTOGRAPHIC COLLECTION, JWH00040.

boomtowns, although oil and gas usually replace gold as the focus of attention.

From her work as a mining camp prostitute, Fannie Bird was able to channel enough gold into her own purse to embark on her venture in Last Chance Gulch. She worked alone, peddling her own body out of her own house, on her own bit of land, on her own terms. She was the area's first proprietor-prostitute, pioneering a legion of self-determined, Last Chance ladies—Bell Robinson, Fanny Clark, Mary Anne Petch, and Josephine Hensley, to name a few—and setting the stage for women of the red light to apply their social guile and economic might in molding the rough-and-tumble settlement that would eventually become the more refined territorial capital called Helena.

From the earliest days, proprietor-prostitutes commanded the sex industry in this otherwise male-dominated community. Before 1885, when a territorial law was enacted that allowed towns to regulate prostitution, harlots were free to work anywhere in the community. Proprietor-prostitutes initially established houses on centrally located

Five large fires swept through Helena between 1869 and 1874. Chicago Joe and other madams grabbed real estate at low prices after such disasters to grow their businesses. This scene was shot in October 1872, showing the aftermath of the fire that raged on August 23 of that year. PHOTOGRAPH COURTESY OF THE MONTANA HISTORICAL SOCIETY RESEARCH CENTER, 953-427.

Main Street, neighboring the other more legitimate businesses in town. Once the law kicked in, however, Helena's first red light district established itself from the bottom of Reeder's Alley north to where the Blackfoot River Brewery stands today. Most of these early buildings were wooden and laid out cheek to jowl, so fires were a frequent problem. Time and again fires decimated Helena's core, and a few women scooped up destroyed properties for next to nothing, thereby allowing them to amass veritable empires in the skin industry after they rebuilt.

These entrepreneurial women were forces to be reckoned with, and local businessmen understood their importance to the local economy. More than that, they contributed to the social stability of the community. Although these madams were often flush enough to pay with cash on the barrelhead when times were tight, they could also rely on each other as well as on prominent men in the legitimate business community for credit. Some proprietresses were known to pay their debts months ahead of schedule after offering promissory notes that put their furniture, jewelry, clothes, and even undergarments on the line. During particularly harsh economic times, even tight-fisted bankers were known to waive the ladies' substantial debts. These women had clout, and the merchants in the seats of power understood that shutting down the red light district would only hamstring the local economy. In time, however, the consolidation of the district into the hands of a few madams signaled a shift in the industry, paralleling changes in Helena's social structure as it matured from mining camp to self-sufficient city.

By 1868, the gold in Last Chance Gulch was played out for all practical purposes. Prospectors and miners continued to work the hills around the region for both gold and silver, but Helena's economy soon grew to include ancillary industries, such as banking, retail, and agriculture. The 1880s marked a period of considerable change in Helena, and in retrospect appears to have been a crucial period for the town as it established itself as an economically viable and permanent urban community. With the first steel rails running through in 1883 for the Northern Pacific Railway, connecting St. Paul, Minnesota, to the Pacific Coast, followed by the Montana Central Railroad connections to Great Falls and Butte in 1887, commerce expanded, and the population of Helena tripled. A resulting building boom changed the face of the downtown core, with more than thirty stone edifices constructed along the newly illuminated Main Street with its freshly paved walkways. As more families moved in, community leaders implemented more ordinances and regulations. One ordinance in particular banned women from being employed in the recently developed downtown core, a move designed to keep the city center "clean and respectable," at least in the minds of the moralists.

In *No Step Backward: Women and Family on the Rocky Mountain Mining Frontier, Helena, Montana 1865-1900,* Paula Petrik noted, "The pioneer aldermen, uncomfortable with a formal licensing system that would bestow a civic blessing on the skin trade, did not want fancy ladies and their profits to disappear. They desired some measure of social control, but its form was problematic." In other words, the savvy town fathers faced a dilemma. On one hand, regulation and licensing provided security and legitimacy for commerce, but on the other hand, such blatant recognition of an "immoral" industry would hardly pass scrutiny. Not that some of them didn't try. Prominent businessman Marcus Lissner, for example, who built the International Hotel in 1868, wrote an appeal to community members in a *Helena Independent* editorial. He warned that if prostitution were completely driven out of town, "[m]en would go where such women were. Drive them out of town, and in five years there would be a city on the outskirts five times as large as Helena." The best solution, Lissner argued, was to allow the demimonde to exist, and let the women continue to ply their trade in their own section of the city, away from other, legitimate businesses. Lissner's International Hotel would later house one of madam Ida Levy's brothels in the early part of the twentieth century. In essence, Lissner took a typical pragmatic stance, one that frequently appeared in similar circumstances throughout the West. Even today, advocates for decriminalizing prostitution make much the same argument—it is better to legalize and regulate a vice than to outlaw it and create an unregulated black market.

Throughout history, prostitution has existed in a precarious limbo, abided by businessmen and women who see it as an economic expression of an unavoidable human urge, and despised by righteous, often religious men and women who view it as an irredeemable vice to be eliminated entirely. Often a somewhat Faustian bargain has prevailed between the two if only because many people in such communities inevitably—if somewhat delicately—have a foot in both worlds.

In any event, what this bargain meant in Helena, Montana, in the 1880s was that women of the night trade began to develop their own territory from the block between Wood and East Bridge Streets and from Joliet Street over to Clore Street (current-day Park Avenue where Reeder's Alley is today), then running north along Clore Street to Wall Street (where the Blackfeet Brewery now sits). With a booming red light district looming on the edge of its otherwise respectable downtown, Helena won the odious reputation of being dubbed "The City of Prostitutes," with the Wood Street block alone quartering twenty-four boarding houses offering sex to those who were willing to pay. Occasionally, to keep up the appearance of placating the moralists, city officials would sweep through this tenderloin district, handing out citations to the working women, which brought in a fair amount of coin for the city. One *Helena Independent* article dated April 21, 1889, reports in a subtle but critical voice that a municipal court judge presiding over a slew of hearings in a single day "posed like a judicial Hercules as he gathered the shekels from nearly a hundred women." In fact, such municipal ambivalence marked nearly every town in Montana where prostitution flourished. The city coffers swelled from such crackdowns, which pleased the moralists, while those on the other end of the nightstick simply chalked it up to the cost of doing business. From an economist's perspective, the occasional raids and the ensuing fines amounted to a sort of de facto licensing. The city fathers tolerated what the moralists deplored, so long as it was periodically "regulated" to keep everyone satisfied.

But the 1880s witnessed another shift in the way prostitution was practiced. As Helena solidified as a "respectable" community and its log-cabin hurdy-gurdy houses and mud streets gave way to clapboard houses and boulevards, enterprising madams realized a coinciding shift in their target market. They may have been removed from the main streets and relegated to auxiliary neighborhoods, but they still played an important role in the burgeoning new economy. The population was maturing, and the flow of money available for what economists politely call "discretionary spending" was no longer coming from the hands of working-class miners. It was accruing into the hands of an emerging elite who preferred more discreet access to these seductive services. The madams, with typical canniness, adroitly positioned themselves to stay ahead of the market. They understood that affluent customers were inclined to frequent more lavish bordellos, styled after the upscale homes on the west side of town, so the women remodeled and expanded their enterprises accordingly.

Despite the apparent extravagance occasioned by the new direction Helena was taking in the 1880s, it would be a mistake to think that this meant nothing but milk and roses for Helena's ladies of the night. The period of women controlling the industry with occasional community oversight was brief. As Helena's population boomed—

tripled from 1880 to 1887—the landscape of the itinerant miner, the speculative merchant, and the opportunistic prostitute gave way to a more staid community populated by families and stable neighborhoods. By 1890, about 100 women worked out of over thirty houses lining Wood and Clore Streets under the rule of eight madams.

And things began to look grim for the women actually working in these houses. Although Helena had hardly been subjected to a thorough sociological analysis or longitudinal study, few if any records prior to 1886 document a prostitute's death from violence or suicide. But by the turn of the century, sadly, things had changed. The industry began to record physical abuse, logging fatalities from violence and drug overdoses. As the century turned, the industry completely slipped into the hands of men who realized how lucrative the skin trade was. Instead of working for themselves, prostitutes now most often worked for pimps. Their brief watch at the red light helm was over.

The clash between economic and moral interests remained consistent. One 1905 editorial in the *Montana News* argued that the people of Helena were hypocritical because even churchgoing pillars of the community were landlords who profited from prostitution, "living off the sorrows of the inmates." If "respectable" business communities had previously existed in an uneasy but more or less harmonious relationship with prostitution to the acknowledged benefit of the women involved, the arrival of pimps only complicated things and had a measurably negative impact on women.

According to Petrik's study, prostitutes were no longer property owners, and in most cases they no longer even had bank accounts. They rented their establishments in the district from businessmen who exploited them. The results were demoralizing for the women of the tenderloin. "The optimism that had characterized Helena's demimonde . . . had given way to sadness," writes Petrik. "Whoring no longer held out even the illusion of opportunity for those who occupied the few places at the top of Wood Street's hierarchy, the possibility of escape into a better life dimmed."

With the coming of the First World War, a small handful of entrepreneurial women did succeed in making a name for themselves with their houses of ill repute in Helena. Two of them remain in popular memory even today—Ida Levy and Big Dorothy. They withstood the changing business climate and shift toward more paternalistic control of the industry, mainly because they were keen businesswomen with a strong social sense who had unique leverage in the community. Several other madams linger on the rolls of local history as well.

CHICAGO JOE—
FIERY QUEEN OF THE RED LIGHT DISTRICT

The fire raging through Helena's Main Street on Valentine's Day in 1869 was a fitting backdrop for the nuptials between Josephine Airey and her beau, Albert Hankins. The fire burned hot and fast, fueled by the timbers of log cabins and flimsy wooden shanties, which were further inflamed by winds swirling down through two gulches into town.

When the inferno finally subsided, Main Street entrepreneurs sifted through the ashes and found that property losses totaled $75,000. Fortunately, the newly married Josephine, a madam known as Chicago Joe, did not suffer any losses with her Bridge Street dance hall; she did, however, use the very next fire that raged through Helena that spring to her advantage. She purchased damaged property on the corner of Wood and Main Streets for four dollars, turning it over for a profit hours later when she sold it to a fellow proprietor-prostitute for $150. She and her new husband took the proceeds and rushed off to White Pine, Nevada, a boom-and-bust silver mining town.

Born in Ireland in 1844, Chicago Joe started life innocently enough as Mary Welch. She came to the United States when she was fourteen, her parents hopeful that their daughter would have a better life than her impoverished homeland could offer, which, because of the infamous potato blight and the notorious absentee landlords, was suffering through one of its most harrowing periods. Whatever wretched poverty she had witnessed in Ireland, the scene was perhaps slightly less desperate in the immigrant neighborhoods of New York City where she worked long hours in sweatshops.

By the time Mary was eighteen, she realized that she needed to make a drastic change in her life in order to get ahead. Her pitiful wages would have been hardly enough to survive on, and the conditions in which she worked had to be taking their toll. Still, at eighteen,

A savvy businesswoman, Josephine Airey, aka Josephine Hensley or Chicago Joe,
was a prominent and wealthy madam in Helena's early years.
C. W. CARTER PHOTOGRAPH COURTESY OF THE MONTANA HISTORICAL SOCIETY RESEARCH CENTER, 944-615.

she had the youthful exuberance and fortitude to make a new start. The sweatshops had not erased her devil-may-care sense of adventure, nor her ambitious appetite for a better life that had guided her to leave Ireland, and so she took what savings she had managed to set aside and purchased a ticket for a train heading to the Midwest.

She got off the train in Chicago, where among the first things she did was change her name to Josephine Airey. Perhaps she thought "Mary Welch" was now too prim or plain, and the new name had a better ring, or perhaps she wanted to completely drop her old life and simply start afresh. Most likely, she felt the need to distance herself from her devout Catholic family and didn't want to leave a trail as she entered a life of prostitution. Josephine was a proud name—the name of Napoleon Bonaparte's wife—and "Airey" had a flowing, light sound, full of lilt and promise.

The 1862 *Chicago City Directory* indicates Josephine Airey resided that year on Wells Street, which happened to be the longest-standing red light district in the Chicago area. It also happened to lie just around the corner from Lou Harper's notorious house of ill repute, known throughout Cooke County as "The Mansion." Wells Street was also only a ten-minute walk to another famous high-society brothel run by prominent Chicago madam Carrie Watson, where twenty-five of the most beautiful women in the city worked. These two prominent madams likely became Josephine's eventual Windy City connection for recruiting attractive new faces to work in her Helena establishments.

Far more important to the fate of Josephine Airey was her residence on Wells Street, which happened to be just a few minutes' walk from the aptly named Hairtrigger Block, one of the city's most popular gambling hot spots in the 1860s. Among the likely regulars in this den of illicit activity with whom Josephine crossed paths was a fellow named Al Hankins—her future husband. It's not clear whether their initial romance sparked up in the seedy neighborhoods of Chicago, or whether they were simply old friends realizing mutual affections once they met up again in the Montana Territory.

We know Josephine Airey left Chicago in 1865, but we can only surmise the reason. Quite possibly, she'd simply had enough of

Chicago's red light district as its ranks swelled. Or she may have decided to follow her lover Al Hankins, who had preceded her to the new territory. On the other hand, perhaps she left Chicago to get away from that dysfunctional relationship, only to rekindle it when they met up again in Helena. According to one 1896 *Anaconda Standard* article that quotes the *Chicago Chronicle*, while still in Chicago, Josephine "gave him her money. Then she pawned her jewels and he took the money she received on them. Her wardrobe went next and he was the beneficiary of the money received on that." In this account, she went west after she had been "plucked and fleeced by the Chicago alderman." Whatever the case, the two eventually tied the knot on that fateful Valentine's Day in Helena. About a year after Josephine ran off to White Pines, Nevada, with her betrothed, she returned to Last Chance Gulch, alone, quite possibly because Al Hankins had burned her one too many times.

Josephine first arrived at Last Chance Gulch in 1865, just three years after the start of the Montana gold rush and a scant year into the local bonanza. The town's population was likely over 4,000 at the time. Main Street bustled with wagons and horses while auctioneers shouted their wares, trying to drown out the calls of their competitors ten feet away on either side. Town was flush with saloons that helped drain the pockets of prospectors. According to one local reporter's account, a person couldn't look at a fellow for less than 25 cents a beer. Prices inflated exponentially as goods were brought in by carriage via the perilous trek from Salt Lake or Fort Benton.

Throughout the West, wherever waves of fortune-seekers came washing up, the men vastly outnumbered the women in a community. Josephine's years in Chicago had made her a savvy entrepreneur, and she intended to exploit that gender disparity to her advantage. Using what cash she had brought with her from Chicago, she bought and fixed up a one-story log cabin on Wood Street, a main business thoroughfare. She hired a small orchestra and a few attractive women and opened up the second dance hall in town—the first to be owned by a woman. Among the early female arrivals in this muddy mining town, she understood that a woman would never be at a loss for money wherever men were hungry for a woman's touch. And her

Chicago experiences taught her what was required to beat out her less refined competition.

To begin, although she was the owner, dance hall manager, and waitress, she also worked alongside her employees, offering herself to those men who wanted more than a dance or a meal. Part of her enduring charm for both her employees and her clients was that she was not above conducting the same business for which she employed others, and she eventually earned respect as a madam who never lost sight of what being a prostitute actually entailed.

It wasn't long before she squirreled away enough money to really start making a name for herself. Soon, everyone in town knew the new quick-witted gal with the native Irish brogue. She was rough around the edges, and could hardly lay claim to being a natural beauty. But what she lacked in good looks she far more than made up for with her engaging charm, and her clients and her employees found her immeasurably appealing. It didn't take long before everyone knew this young businesswoman from Chicago, resulting in a nickname that would stick with her for the rest of her life: Chicago Joe.

According to one newspaper account, Chicago Joe started her own dance hall because she wanted to run an "honest" business, without all the violence and crime associated with the typical establishment as frequented by more salacious types. She once suggested, in her characteristically amusing style, that she didn't want any robberies on her premises—no one was to be bound, gagged, or beaten before having their pockets emptied.

Meanwhile, Al Hankins was also making a name for himself in the Montana Territory, if somewhat ignominiously. According to an article in the *Chicago Tribune,* Hankins and his brothers were identified as members of the "Regulators," a group formed in retaliation and in contempt of the Vigilance Committee. Especially vicious, they declared that "every man hung by the vigilantes would result in five men hanging," a policy referred to as the "Five to One billet." More interested in filthy lucre than any principled resistance to the vigilantes, Hankins and his ilk were among the worst of the criminals, robbing and killing innocent men for quick financial gain. What was worse, they masqueraded as legitimate law enforcement, robbing their victims and often hanging them, but afterward attaching placards to the corpses that identified the victim as "a pickpocket" or "thief."

Another account, corroborated by court records from Anaconda, identified Hankins as having swindled an ex-lover, one Anna Belsford from Deer Lodge, out of $2,000. Elsewhere, Hankins was mentioned as the prime suspect in the robbery of a Blackfoot City brothel, where $4,000 had gone missing. (Blackfoot City no longer exists, but at the time was located a little more than twelve miles southwest of Marysville, not far from Helena.) Was Chicago Joe aware of any of these rumors of her paramour? If she knew, she apparently didn't care. He was handsome, he was charming, and he had his good points. Hankins was a philosophical fellow who quoted poetry and waxed thoughtfully, using words most of the miners in town could hardly pronounce. He was a lover of horses, a capable rider, and a man physically fit with an athletic build who dressed like a gentleman. He and Joe shared a love for the fancy life and fine food and drink.

Naturally, one puzzles over her lack of foresight. Surely she knew her lover was a crook and a thief with a sordid past, and it couldn't have been too much of a surprise when he plied his trade on his own wife. Perhaps she was fooled by the illusion of love forged in the coals of mutual vice. Or maybe she imagined that a new start in a new region would provide an opportunity to rise above past transgressions, offering a chance for a more conventional "happily ever after." Whatever had lulled her into the marriage soon proved to have been a sham.

Hankins eventually returned to Chicago to become the owner of one of the illustrious, high-end gambling houses known for its shady dealings. There is not much information on the intervening years to provide a full understanding of what passed between them, but this much is certain: Al Hankins apparently bilked his wife of a considerable sum of money. (One might say sweet justice was served when he met his fate one morning by suffocating in a folded-up Murphy bed.)

Chicago Joe was a woman who learned from her experiences, resilient, never letting adverse circumstances defeat her and using apparent setbacks to her advantage. Much wiser and with a hardened heart, from then on, she played her hand a little closer to her chest.

Their Valentine's Day wedding, after all, had been overshadowed by the raging fire that same day, which ruined the business district and prompted Joe and Hankins' move to Nevada. But she had come through ahead. And that was not the only fire to destroy businesses in the little frontier town. When she returned to Helena from Nevada in 1871, the gold had all but run out, and about 1,000 fewer people now called the place home. An October fire raging through the business district provided her another opportunity to come out ahead. Once again she scooped up damaged properties at low prices, setting into motion the birth of her red light empire. By 1874, Chicago Joe had acquired a considerable amount of property.

Meanwhile, the bitter sting of Al Hankins had worn off, and Joe married again, this time to local gambler James "Black Hawk" Hensley. He, too, was handsome, svelt, and loved gambling. While she trusted him enough to fall in love and take his name, and to find him dependable and comforting through hard times, she was careful to make sure that only her name, and her name alone, appeared on the legal deeds to her business ventures.

In fact, in a revealing footnote to their odd union, Chicago Joe caused a few chuckles when she posted notices in the local papers between 1882 and 1883, informing anyone who served her husband a drink or allowed him to sit at the gambling table that they could expect "swift and forceful prosecution," because she preemptively denied all financial obligations for his debts and behaviors.

In 1875, she and Hensley built what would be remembered as one of Helena's most famous prostitution houses and dance halls, the Red Light Saloon, an event that coincided with her becoming the largest landowner in the red light district. Chicago Joe also owned and operated other establishments, including a bordello called the Grand and the Coliseum Variety Theatre, which alone cost $30,000 to build.

Part of Hensley's success may be attributed to the wisdom of choosing to act as her own manager. Her early experiences with the trade in Chicago had taught her that human beings in general were avaricious, but especially so around liquor and the sex trade. She was illiterate, but she knew how to read people, and she could count and keep track of money and receipts. She inventoried her own liquor

The Grand, shown here circa 1935, stood at 34 East State Street in Helena.
U.S. GEOLOGICAL SURVEY PHOTOGRAPH COURTESY OF THE SEAN LOGAN COLLECTION.

stocks, hired the music and dance talent herself, and watched the flow of money with a careful eye. Her establishments were popular and always packed and busy, but she made sure to keep an eye on the performances in the theatre. At the end of each, she plied the clientele and encouraged them to engage her girls' services.

Joe possessed consummate charm and exuded charisma, and miners and cowboys alike deferred to her. One observer remarked, "She could sell $100 worth of champagne while one of her company was wheedling a man to buy a pint of beer." She was also well known for her lavish and impeccable taste in dress; one contemporary described her as often wearing a gown of green velvet sporting a train so long that she carried it wrapped in two or three folds about her forearm. The effect was highlighted by her choice of high collars of pink lace, the entire ensemble set off with glittering jewelry, including gold wrist bangles studded with glistening diamonds.

The opulence of her person was matched by the magnificence of her businesses. An *Independent Record* article in 1884 noted that she had improved her dance hall, adding a fifty-foot extension (two stories of brick) for the sum of $3,000, and had erected a two-story frame building on Wood Street for $1,000. Taking advantage of Montana's new railroad connections to the rest of the country, and her connections to the consummate madams of the Midwest, Joe arranged for the scheduled arrival of fresh faces, and she began importing new dance hall girls from her old stomping grounds. Business boomed.

But this success was not without its hurdles, with 1885 proving to be a difficult year. It did provide, however, another occasion for the resolute Chicago Joe to triumph. The local government passed laws attempting to ban the existence of the "hurdy-gurdy" houses, and naturally she was the first object of their prosecution. According to *Independent Record* journalist Terence Corrigan, "Joe was successful in her work as a madam in Helena, despite the Montana Legislature's unsuccessful attempts to outlaw her profession with an attempt to legislate morals in 1885." One of the prosecuting attorneys derided her with a rhetorical flourish characteristic of the age, when he said her businesses were "establishments wherein men's souls are lured to the shores of sin by the combined seductive influences of wine, women and dance."

She hired a smooth-talking lawyer to defend her, who presented an argument based purely on semantics. Since "hurdy-gurdy" referred to a musical instrument and connoted merely a dance hall wherein such music was provided, his client could hardly be accused, let alone convicted, of any moral transgression.

Nevertheless, the prudish lawyers eventually had their day in court and succeeded in shutting down the red light district, at least to the eye of the casual observer. With characteristic canniness and guile, Chicago Joe endured, mainly by retrofitting her dance hall as a "variety theater," but still making "personal services" discreetly available. When the Coliseum was refurbished in response to the 1885 crackdown, a notice in the local paper announced its grand reopening:

The Coliseum Concert hall will be opened to public. The Dance hall of the Coliseum theater has been refitted and neatly arranged for concert purposes. Mrs. Hensley will make it a point to engage only vocalists and musicians of acknowledged ability, and of dancers she will secure the services of the very best now appearing in concert and vaudeville. The best of order will be rigorously maintained at all times and those with leisure time on their hands can while away an hour at the Coliseum Concert hall very pleasantly.

Crowds lined up around the corner of the Coliseum for Joe's shows. According to an article in the *Anaconda Standard,*

The gallery was divided into stalls, in which men armed to the teeth sat and drank and smoked, and drowned the noise labeled as much which was occasionally heard on the stage. Into these stalls went women who were stupefied with the liquor of the town, or who stupefied the men with it and then robbed them. The "talent" of the theater had the privilege of visiting these stalls between their "acts," and as they were trained in their business the stage often waited for some songster or dancer to appear while she was lingering in a stall fleecing her besotted victim of the last penny. Beer sold for $1 a pint, and a poisonous decoction labeled champagne was $5 a pint. In order that the "talent" might be induced to dispose of champagne in preference to beer the woman was allowed 20 per cent commission on each pint of wine.

Joe hit yet another roadblock in 1887, with a court battle that resulted in forbidding the sale of liquor in hurdy-gurdy houses. Her ingenious work-around? Cutting a hole through the wall into her old dance hall and selling liquor surreptitiously. The case wound its way to the state supreme court, which decided that her "hurdy-gurdy" house didn't legally fall under the law in question, so she closed the passageway to her old dance hall and reopened the bars at the theater.

Throughout the 1880s, Chicago Joe triumphed and established an enduring reputation as a powerful member of the community who wielded enormous political power. In the words of an *Anaconda Standard* article, "When Joe passed word that a candidate was to be slaughtered, it usually happened that he was." In retaliation to the trouble caused by the statesman who tried to shut down her hurdy-gurdy house, Joe personally canvassed door-to-door to oppose his campaign for political office, essentially killing any hopes he had for a win.

On the other hand, Chicago Joe was magnanimous, paying passage from Ireland for many of her relatives, whom she helped set up in businesses of their own, and she paid for the education of some of their children. (According to one source, she also had two daughters, possibly a son, but there's no mention of her maintaining any relational ties with any of them, other than in providing financial support.) She was also known for loaning money to fellow prostitutes in need of help, who often failed to make good on their debts. In 1889, when news arrived of the devastating Johnstown Flood in Pennsylvania, according to the *Independent Record,* Chicago Joe pledged the night's receipts from the Coliseum to relief for the victims.

Eventually, however, she overextended herself, as did many businesses leading up to the financial collapse and Panic of 1893, which was brought about in large part by the repeal of the Sherman Silver Purchase Act. Chicago Joe found herself compelled to sell all of her properties but the Red Light Saloon, which she renamed the Red Star. According to historian and scholar Paula Petrik, Chicago Joe began to run into financial difficulties as early as 1890, when she was forced to approach local millionaire Thomas Cruse for assistance. Cruse had struck his own fortune in 1876 at Marysville, with the profitable Drumlummon mine, and had many business dealings with women of the demimonde. At one point, Joe had mortgaged over $6,000 of property to Thomas Cruse's savings bank. She also found herself indebted to wholesale liquor merchant Jacob Switzer, who loaned her $10,000 against her Wood Street properties. By 1896, the wolf was unavoidably at the door, and Joe was compelled to liquidate everything to Switzer. According to Petrik, the madam had gambled that the financial panic of 1893 would damage Cruse, if not bankrupt him, thereby relieving her of her debt. But Cruse was shrewd and was in fact one of the few local financiers to make it through the panic relatively unscathed. He sued to recover his debts, and Joe—recognizing her defeat—did not even show up for her court date. She lost nearly all of her property and wealth to receivership and spent the last few years of her life in debt, far removed from the fantastic wealth she had once enjoyed.

Chicago Joe Hensley died in 1899, at age fifty-six, from pneumonia.

Her funeral was a celebrated, sumptuous affair. Governor Toole's brother led the procession through town, and the celebration of her life and contributions was immortalized in the local newspapers, featuring many eulogies and kind encomia from the locals who adored and revered her.

In a tribute to and in recognition of her contributions to the Helena community, and as a fitting symbol of her redemption from what might have been a tarnished reputation, Chicago Joe found her final resting place in the Old Saint Mary's Catholic Cemetery in Helena.

Fannie Spencer— The Polyamorous Proprietress

Arriving in Helena sometime between 1867 and 1871, Fannie Spencer was a young, up-and-coming proprietor-prostitute who showed promise for success. Thanks to one of Helena's preeminent madams, Louisa Couselle, Fannie was able to borrow the funds necessary to purchase her second property, a few blocks to the west of her Bridge Street house. She leased at least one of her properties out to another local prostitute, Blanche Emerson. Varying accounts make it unclear whether she prostituted herself out of her other property, or whether she actually had a bordello with hired women working under her. Whatever the case, she had a plan—she was positioning herself to reign over the next era of women working the burgeoning demimonde district along Clore Street. Unfortunately, a premature death prevented her from ever realizing her goal.

It is hard to be sure of who, exactly, Fannie Spencer was. She constantly equivocated about her age, her origin, and her marital status, distancing herself further and further from her roots—and from her father's own final, dying request.

She was born in 1845 in Nauvoo, Illinois, a town purchased by Mormons and renamed by their prophet, Joseph Smith, after he led a group there on a vision quest to escape religious persecution in Missouri. Fannie's family moved westward from there when she was two years old after her father, Hyrum Spencer, had taken to heart the calling of Brigham Young and became one of the first followers to slog the Mormon Pioneer Trail to Salt Lake City. Exhausted from the strain of six days' travel in the heat of summer, the forty-eight-year-old Hyrum stopped his steed in Iowa, near Mount Pisgah. It was late afternoon, and he asked his nephew to assist him in dismounting; he claimed he could continue no further. Seven hours later, Hyrum lay dead on the side of the trail after muttering his final words, "Say to my family, live and die with this work."

Left with nine children, Fannie's mother remarried, this time to Fannie's uncle, Daniel, who would later become one of the Mormon Church's greatest advocates for polygamy. Although Elizabeth was his only wife when the two joined hands, he eventually took on three other wives, much to Elizabeth's chagrin. Fannie grew up in a polygamist household that was devout, yet rife with strain and resentment.

When she came of age, she fell in love with Isaac Fordonski, who was a heathen in the eyes of her clan—he was, after all, a gentile and a liberal idealist in both politics and philosophy—quite the contrast to what Fannie had been surrounded with her entire life. The two married when she was twenty years old. Two years later, quite likely fleeing the high-handedness of Fannie's zealous tribe, the young couple headed to Virginia City, Montana, after hearing about the promise of the rich placer strikes in Alder Gulch.

The gold rush to Alder Gulch happened fast on the heels of the earlier strikes at Bannack and Virginia City. One group of travelers on their way to Bannack discovered the riches in Alder Gulch quite by accident. One of the men thought he'd give a go at sifting a pan of dirt and was surprised with shimmering results. He'd scooped $1.75 worth of precious metal, and the group found promising colors at other nearby points. The men staked off several claims in the area and then raced to Bannack to stock up on provisions before heading back to begin the hard work of harvesting their treasure. Word spread, and what followed was the usual stampede of prospectors flooding into the gulch, jockeying for strikes of their own.

One of the prospectors in that initial Alder Gulch crew, Barney Hughes, placer mined until his luck waned and then moved to Virginia City, seeking work. He landed there around the same time that the Fordonskis settled in. Barney was a handsome gentleman, one of the most popular young chaps in the territory, and he quickly secured a job as manager of the local telegraph office. Although she was married, the winsome Fannie Fordonski was taken by his charm and striking profile, and the feeling was apparently reciprocated. It wasn't long before their mutual attraction became a full-fledged affair, which persisted for some time before it was finally discovered.

One afternoon, hubby Isaac came home earlier than expected, only to find his bride bundled under the covers with the strapping Hughes. Heartbroken and outraged, the cuckold beat a hasty retreat to Bozeman, where he made a name for himself opening a tonsorial parlor, plunging into political activism, and tinkering around with inventions that he would subsequently patent. He filed for divorce in 1871.

Barney Hughes also left Alder Gulch when some pals offered him a grubstake in the remote Big Hole River Valley. Fannie had been fun, but he was a bachelor and free spirit at heart and so opted to live in solitude and hope for another lucky strike.

Fannie was left alone, with neither husband nor lover. Without many other options available to her, she headed to Helena, where she fell into a life of prostitution. She became a belle in the Clore Street district, one of the figures responsible for its demographic shift from a primarily Chinese district, which had no record of women-run prostitution businesses, to one with a considerable number of white proprietor-prostitutes.

"Live and die with this work," her father had said, breathing his last breath and leaving his young daughter Fannie to eventually fend for herself in the West. He would likely have rolled over in his unmarked grave had he known what his daughter was to become. But she did, in fact, take his words to heart in a sense. One might say her zealous, polygamous upbringing set the stage for Fannie partaking in a zealous polyandry-ing of sorts. She set her sights for greatness, only to die suddenly at the young age of thirty-six, leaving her Clore Street property and substantial debt.

She did live and die with her work, just as her father had requested, although it likely wasn't the work he'd had in mind.

Mollie Byrnes—
Crazy Belle of the Tenderloin

Had she known her elegant State Street home overlooking downtown Helena would eventually become a somewhat run-down tenement in a low-rent district, Mollie Byrnes may have burst into tears. Either that, or she may have wielded her knife at whoever was responsible for letting it go to shambles.

A New Orleans native, Mollie arrived in Helena during the summer of 1880, looking to reap the benefits of the rivers of gold flowing from miners' pockets. She was a "summer woman," one of the many ladies who swooped into town during the summer months, when the mines were operating in full swing, to troll for men who were loose with their cash. When the winter months approached, miners became less inclined to spend their earnings, but a summer woman could easily leave town with $500 in her purse—and in a good summer, maybe even a $1,000. Keep in mind this was after she had spent a considerable sum on the costs of living and doing business. According to Paula Petrik's account in *No Step Backward*, "Women in the demimonde had expenses to consider: they paid rent, medical, grocery, and liquor bills; indulged themselves in fine furniture and related household items, furs, expensive clothing, and jewelry; and probably paid bribes to local lawmen." Even so, a halfway responsible prostitute could bank a respectable sum at the end of the working season.

Mollie took her surplus earnings and left after her first summer, but, recognizing her potential for wealth in the territory's capital, she returned for good the following year to set up shop, under the name Belle Crafton, in Helena's tenderloin district. She made a killing, depositing as much as $50 a day into her bank account, building enough savings to start investing in property in earnest. She purchased a saloon on Joliet Street, right next door to the Red Star Saloon, owned by heavy player Chicago Joe. By 1886, she had firmly secured her position as one of the top three proprietresses of Helena's red light empire when she mortgaged everything she had to finance the construction of a $12,000 bordello, called The Castle, on the northeast corner of Joliet and State Streets, across from Chicago Joe's brothel, the Grand. By the 1880s, of course, the short-lived boom of the gold years had passed, but the city of Helena had proved it had staying power. As the community solidified into a stable city, the market in prostitution shifted from rough-and-tumble hurdy-gurdy girls entertaining scruffy miners to high-class women catering to a clientele that included city fathers and pillars of the community. Belle decorated her new bordello with extravagant furnishings, and she staffed it with the most beautiful women she could hire. Her clientele found themselves comfortably seated in the lap of luxury, while as many as seven resident beauties tended to the men's every desire.

Although the madam firmly established her reputation as one of the top three dignitaries in Helena's red light district, despite her elegant éclat, she also earned a nickname she would just as soon forget: Crazy Belle. Everyone recognized she was a woman to avoid when agitated—especially when armed with a weapon. She once pulled a revolver on prominent businessman C. L. Vawter, for example, and promised to send him to his "heavenly reward." On another occasion, she was arrested for brandishing a blade at one of her women, whom she had shipped in from the east to work in The Castle, but who soon began to put on airs. Not long after the poor young woman arrived, their personalities clashed, with Belle having little patience for her new employee's contemptuous attitude.

One time, Crazy Belle suffered the harsh consequences of her own temper when confronted with a local carpetbagger, Michael A. Meyendorff. He was a man of Polish roots, a former secretary of the Territorial Republican Committee and the superintendent of the Helena Episcopal Church Sunday school. After making the rounds at numerous Wood Street cathouses one evening, he was well sauced by the time he ventured into Belle's place. Once there, he continued his boozing, and his loud-mouthed blathering caused more disturbances with each additional drink. Belle grabbed the belligerent sot by the ear and dragged him out onto the street. As noted in an August 1883 account in the *Benton Weekly Record*, Belle's actions drove Meyendorff to "[e]jaculating a nine-jointed oath in choice Polish," and he rushed to a nearby police officer to demand the madam's arrest. The officer headed into Crazy Belle's establishment to read her rights, when, in a moment of questionable judgment, "the wild Slavonic spirit of

Meyendorff boiled over, and he proceeded to smite Miss Crafton."
He let loose and started pounding her in tooth and jaw, leaving Belle
bloodied, her mouth looking, according to the *Record*, "like the crater
of an extinct volcano." After spending a day in the dentist's chair, Belle
demanded Meyendorff compensate her for the repair work, and she
settled on $175 to avoid going to court in a civil suit—and to avoid any
more bad press in the local papers.

Perhaps Crazy Belle's *nom de guerre* was indicative of how stress-
ful it was to be a major player in Helena's nightlife. Or perhaps her
moments of rage were a result of discontentment with her lot in life.
In any event, she decided she'd had enough living a life of turpitude
and began to make some real changes in earnest. She had built her
empire with her sights set on a peaceful life outside of the tenderloin,
and her business decisions reflected her desire to secure a life of refinement and respectability some distance from her life of disrepute.

But not *too* much of a distance.

Soon after purchasing her saloon next to Chicago Joe's Red
Star, she sold it to a lawyer acquaintance, signing her name as Belle
Crafton, only to buy it back from the same friend minutes later using
her birth name, Mollie Byrnes. She proceeded to sell off her other
red light properties, then purchased various residential properties
throughout town. She held onto The Castle, however, and built a
residence two blocks farther east, outside of the tenderloin on the
other side of Warren Street. She decorated her new home lavishly
with plush drapes, patterned wallpaper, heirloom tables, ornate side-
boards, chandeliers, and imported tapestries—echoing in every detail
her *maison de joie* a few doors down. Both buildings, inside and out,
displayed Belle's taste for the finest accoutrements money could buy.

Belle's new home, with its location in such close proximity to her
bordello, succinctly summed up the reality of her existence. She ju-
diciously extended the toes of one foot to tap into a semblance of respectability, while her other foot remained steadfastly planted in the
still hard, and deceptively refined, tenderloin.

During her pursuit for decency, like many women of her trade,
Belle was repeatedly exploited in matters of the heart. She married
a local salesman in 1890, Thomas Butler Eddingfield, who was four

years her junior. They settled into her new home on State Street, quite comfortable with the new living arrangement. Soon after, Belle opted to lease The Castle to another madam, Lillie Ashton, to distance herself even more from her old life. But the couple's matrimonial bliss was short-lived. Thomas was, perhaps, a little too comfortable with his new living situation. He borrowed large sums of money from Belle for business ventures that never came to fruition. He squandered the couple's land holdings through losses incurred by rowdy living and heavy drinking. And when he was drunk, he was mean, calling her a "low shanty Irish" and physically beating her. The final blow came when he struck her on the head, inflicting permanent injury. Belle had had enough. Eight years after they wed, she petitioned for divorce.

Less than a month after the breakup, she returned to the altar with another paramour, William Weinsheimer, who put up a front of being a wealthy cattleman. Theirs was a rocky relationship from the get-go. She found out that the man she fell in love with was not a wealthy cattleman after all. He actually entered into their union with nothing—only a desire to benefit from his wife's affluence. As her new husband's true nature began to emerge, Belle began revisiting her previous lover. Once again, she found herself straddling two lives— married to William but proceeding to rendezvous with Thomas on occasion. Perhaps they reminisced and commiserated as old friends, or perhaps they had more amorous trysts. Whatever the case, she was soon reminded of why her relationship with Thomas hadn't worked out in the first place.

One day she visited his office, and the two shared a discussion over cocktails. Thomas purportedly doped her drink, convincing the benumbed Belle to sign a will leaving him a portion of her property should she pass before he did. It wasn't until a month later that she learned he had actually filed a deed to the Clerk and Recorder's Office, rendering him the new owner of half her personal property, which was now worth around $30,000. An enraged Belle took him to court, claiming she'd been duped and would never have knowingly consented to such an agreement. The court ruled in Belle's favor, and the deed was voided.

Belle had her property back, but not her pride. The case had made national news—a *New York Times* account of the dispute reported she had been incapable of having "the proper physical and mental condition to transact business."

In a last desperate attempt to gain her foothold on a life of respectability, Belle sold The Castle, washing her hands clean of the tenderloin altogether and severing her last connection to the red light life. And then she spiraled into depression.

Still stuck in her second bad marriage, Belle proceeded to fall hard into the bottle. Within a year, forty-two-year-old Belle was dead from acute alcoholism—three days after signing a will that entitled her current husband, William Weinsheimer, to her entire estate, now diminished to $20,000.

What is perhaps most troubling about the will is that she had been incapable of signing her own name that day, either too drunk or sick to sign properly. Instead, she marked the papers with an X, which alarmed her relatives down in New Orleans. Belle's half-brother, James Byrnes, filed a lawsuit claiming Weinsheimer was a con man who never truly loved his wife. In court, James argued his late sister had been physically and emotionally abused by the "shiftless, worthless adventurer," and he presented witnesses who claimed a previous will existed that gave Belle's entire estate over to her two nieces, James' daughters. He even went so far as to accuse Weinsheimer of murdering Belle with drink. But James' plea fell on deaf ears, and the court awarded Weinsheimer the entire estate.

Today, at the tail end of a nondescript block of what is now State Street in Helena, Montana, you can see the red brick house with elegant turrets that was Mollie Byrnes' house and the remnant of her last attempt to break completely free of the tenderloin and give up her life as a woman of ill repute. Whether her failure to disengage can be attributed to bad luck or poor choices, or an unfortunate combination of the two, the fact is Mollie Byrnes could never quite disentangle herself from her past or the life she had chosen, no matter how earnestly she tried to reinvent herself. And though she had been a colorful character who made headlines in her day, in the end, she died an alcoholic, unhappy in love, and still living a few blocks from the life she desperately tried to leave.

IDA LEVY—LILACS AND BACKDOORS

Anyone who has experienced Helena, Montana, in springtime will surely have been partially anesthetized by the fragrance of lilacs. A particularly beautiful and hardy shrub, the common lilac—*Syringa vulgaris*—is not native to Montana, nor to North America for that matter, but was brought west by pioneers and shoved into the ground with the hope of making their rough new homesteads more hospitable, more like the old homes they left behind. These plants persevered—thrived, in fact—in the harsh climes of the Rocky Mountain West. Their hardiness matched the optimism and determination of the early immigrants, marking their first efforts at permanence in a new land with a pleasant, domestic fragrance. These lilacs even outlasted the settlers, enduring long after those who planted them had passed on.

Montana's premier first lady, Lily Toole, wife of the state's first governor, Joseph K. Toole, brought the gift of *Syringa* to Helena in the 1890s. Toole transplanted lilacs from her home state of Ohio, placing them in the yard of the first couple's home on Rodney Street. Eventually, Lily was responsible for arranging the landscaping at the state capitol, and she insisted that lilacs be planted all around the grounds. Sadly, these original shrubs on the capitol grounds have succumbed to the vagaries of time and subsequent landscapers, but their remnants persist in the Rodney Street yard to this day. Even more impressively, clippings from her original plantings have been passed around through the years and propagated in nearly every neighborhood in town. Thanks in large part to Lily Toole's early efforts, spring in Helena every year brings billowing pillows of purple and white that border walkways throughout the capital's historic neighborhoods, their essence peaking in the warmth of the afternoon sun and settling like ambrosial gossamer on the olfactories of her citizens.

In literature and song, lilacs, like roses, are intimately associated with love. Scientists emphasize the incredible power of scent in memory, especially the recall of emotional memories. Like roses, lilacs recall the passionate courage of first love. Springtime is the season for lovers, and among the dominant notes of a spring evening, at least in Helena, is the omnipresent odor of the lilac. But as pervasive as the lilac bush may be, its lusty blooms are fleeting. They last only two or three weeks before they drop their florets, leaving behind heart-leafed afterthoughts to the bold proclamations of summer's advances.

A lilac's scent emerges from a complex potion of organic compounds, one of which happens to be a chemical called indole, found also in flowers like gardenia, jasmine, and honeysuckle. Trace amounts of indole can produce a gorgeous blast that triggers a libidinal response in anyone who sniffs it. Flowers really are romantic, because their fragrances put us in the mood for love. The whole fragrance industry revolves around crafting indole-infused solutions aimed at elevating human desire. But in one of nature's baffling ironies, this substance, in its most concentrated form, is the very same that puts the fetor of decay in coal tar and the sulphury funk in human flatulence. Indole is produced from the decomposition of tryptophan in the intestines, resulting in the release of some of our most embarrassing odors. Fragrance historian Elena Vosnaki describes isolated indole as having "a musty, weird moth-ball smell that is a little stale, reminiscent of decay, like something has gone off, and you can't really pinpoint what it is."

Helena old-timer Gerald Sullivan remembered how something seemed a little "off" when he was a young teen working at Anderson's Clothing over the holidays in 1944. And it all started with an off-season whiff of lilac.

As Sullivan tells it, he was feeling fortunate to hold a job where the *haute monde* of Helena shopped for their Kuppenheimer suits, Wembley ties, and Irish linen handkerchiefs. On any given day, Sullivan would eavesdrop on casual bull sessions between the regulars who hung out in the store—elected officials, law enforcement agents, lawyers—as they shared news about the war and politics, local gossip, and whatever else was happening about town.

As luck would have it, he happened to be working alone in the store on the last shopping day before Christmas when a short, handsome woman with salt-and-pepper marcelled hair, barely five feet tall, who was bundled in an elegant fur coat, entered through the front door. She wore a high-feathered hat with a veil draped over her eyes and was weighted down with an impressive collection of gem-ridden jewelry. She carried in with her the sweet scent of lilac blooms, which permeated the store, announcing her presence.

Gerald Sullivan knew all about this woman. Everyone in Helena did. From the moment that Prohibition had come to an end, Ida Levy had owned the Silver Dollar Bar, a popular canteen on the ground level of a building called the St. Louis Block, located on South Main Street, in exactly the location of today's popular restaurant, the Windbag Saloon. In 1944, the front door of Ida Levy's establishment may have boasted the Silver Dollar Bar marquee, but it was the door in back that was responsible for her great notoriety.

It was the most popular postern in town, leading upstairs to the place that everyone in town talked about: Ida's Rooms. She even got national recognition when her venue's neon sign, "Ida's Rooms," reportedly appeared in the pages of *Life* magazine. Ida Levy had only recently remodeled the rooms in response to new federal regulations banning the operation of "cribs," or tiny studios, in which prostitutes conducted their business. Cribs were a staple of the industry, and down in Butte the well-known cribs for years had lined Venus Alley. What was formerly a long line of "offices" had been transformed into a collection of five sitting rooms and seven bedrooms where prostitutes could service their clients in relative luxury, at least compared to the cribs.

Sullivan's memories of Levy echoed longtime conventional wisdom in his hometown. It was said that she was a fixture of such prominence in Helena—in the entire state, for that matter—that state legislators felt comfortable holding their caucuses in her upper-level suites.

And Sullivan would soon learn, firsthand, that even the most well-heeled and upright members of the Helena community indulged themselves on occasion, entering through that best-known back door in town to assuage their libidos for a fee.

Now, in Anderson's Clothing, he stood face-to-face with this local celebrity. He apprehensively greeted his customer. Ida was tending to her last-minute Christmas shopping, and she made the point clearly to Gerald that she sought only "the best" items.

"When I say the best," she instructed him, "I mean the one which costs the most money, whether it's the best quality or not."

Ben Barnett rented a storefront from Ida Levy at 21 South Main, next to the madam's Silver Dollar Bar. Ben's two sons, Harry and Norman, fondly remember Ida joining their family for Passover dinner, for which she cooked a mean matzoh ball soup and gefilte fish.
PHOTOGRAPH COURTESY OF NORMAN BARNETT.

On Sullivan's recommendations, Ida purchased a collection of unique—and expensive—items for her gift recipients, including a five X beaver Stetson hat; a gaudy, one-of-a-kind, silk tie displaying a hand-painted rainbow trout; a sky-blue cashmere sweater; and three pairs of the brightest Interwoven argyle socks the store had on hand, with matching garters. Once she was satisfied with her selections, she asked the boy to wrap each of her gifts. But before he was allowed to seal them up, she pulled out a small bottle from her handbag and ceremoniously anointed each individual package with a spritz of lilac essence.

When she had made her purchases, Ida asked Sullivan to call her a cab and have it meet her at the rear door. Her final request was for him to lean over, so she could give him a quick peck on the cheek and place a ten-spot in his palm before exiting out back. Relieved to have lived through the experience without too much shame and his manhood still intact, Sullivan didn't think much more about it and went on to enjoy his own holiday celebration over the next couple of days.

But Ida was not far from his mind when he returned to the store the day after Christmas. His work shift began like any other day, with the regulars coming in to share a smoke and the latest scuttlebutt. As Sullivan mopped the floor, he asked the gentlemen to lift their feet, so he could clean the area beneath them. As the men obliged, Sullivan noticed that the socks and garters of the justice of the peace happened to match exactly a set Sullivan had sold to Ida during her shopping jaunt the day before Christmas. Before Sullivan himself had a chance to blush, in came the chief of police, who happened to have on an impressive and striking sky-blue cashmere sweater under his police jacket—exactly like the one Ida had purchased! As if to clinch his suspicions, Sullivan detected the unmistakable scent of lilacs when the man walked by.

Later that afternoon, one of Helena's most successful attorneys came in, wearing the one-of-a-kind silk tie that Sullivan had personally wrapped for Ida. And to cap off the queue of clandestine Lotharios, in sauntered the sheriff, just before closing time, to admire his brand-new, five X beaver Stetson hat in the store's three-way mirror. Naturally, Sullivan identified it as precisely the hat Ida Levy had purchased in that very store a week earlier.

Ida Levy had a reputation for her tongue-in-cheek approach to gift giving. One account tells how she once purchased an entire case of bright yellow neckties, and whenever prominent community members paid a visit to her premises, she would pull the fellow off to the side, chat him up, and charm him into believing that he was her favorite customer. To prove her sincerity, she would then bestow upon him one of the ties from the lot she had purchased and request that, as an honored guest, he proudly don the neckwear for the New Year's Eve ball held annually at the Civic Center. When the big event rolled round, about half of Helena's most dignified citizens appeared wearing a token of Ida's "personal" adoration, a sea of yellow nearly as damning as Hester Prynne's scarlet letter.

Ida Levy arrived in Helena from New York City in 1913. She came just as Helena was feeling the initial effects of the temperance movement, a force that was working overtime to tame the Wild West. "Moral reform" generated some profound irony in the West for women. On the one hand, the movement was aligned with and helped give birth to the suffrage movement, which was firmly dedicated to securing for women equal rights and the opportunity to control their own lives and livelihoods. Yet on the other hand, by galvanizing public sentiment so effectively against alcohol and prostitution, the temperance movement undermined one of the few existing avenues available at the time for women to realize that control. The issue was complicated by the fact that firebrands like Carrie Nation tended to come from back East, where social mores were profoundly different from the frontier West. Whereas madams in the eastern states might very well have felt marginalized or disparaged, in the West they could be autonomous individuals with unique opportunities for proprietorship, land acquisition, and phenomenal wealth. And Montana held the last vestiges of the Wild West in the early twentieth century. Largely because of its remoteness, Montana has always been difficult to get to (railroads did not enter the territory until the 1880s), and well into the mid-twentieth century, Montana was, in many ways, a decade or so behind the rest of the country.

But Carrie Nation and her temperance movement amassed broad support relatively quickly, and by 1920 Prohibition would quash the legal trade in alcohol for more than a decade. Prostitution had been made illegal in 1917, but the madams worked around the law, reconfiguring their premises as "furnished rooms," without specifying precisely what exactly was being furnished. In Montana, Prohibition arrived even earlier at the state level, two years prior to the national Volstead Act. Pressure was coming to bear from another direction as well: the United States' involvement in World War I. As the nation geared up to engage in the Great War, the military sought to minimize what in those days was among the most debilitating consequences of war, namely the proliferation among the troops of sexually transmitted diseases such as syphilis and gonorrhea. Because prostitution is among the most obvious vectors for transmission of venereal diseases, the federal government actively sought to suppress the trade, which created an enormous problem for women whose livelihoods depended on their ability to solicit sex.

In 1918, Congress passed the Chamberlain-Kahn Act, which modern scholars cite as among the most egregious and intrusive invasions into women's privacy. The act essentially gave medical authorities the power to label any woman with a suspected venereal disease as a prostitute. Even worse, because prostitutes often consorted with soldiers and thereby could transmit the disease, the act further allowed prostitutes to be declared a threat to national security. In fact, any woman walking unescorted down the street could be accused of prostitution and thereupon tossed into jail, with no recourse to a writ of habeas corpus. By the War Department's own estimates, more than 15,000 women were imprisoned under this law.

This advancement of a conservative current pushing communities toward a higher moral ground, coupled with a federal witch hunt to quash syphilis's pernicious spread, effectively shut down Helena's red light district on the edge of town, where other famous Helena madams, including Chicago Joe, Lillie McGraw, and Mollie Byrnes, had openly run their houses. Ever resourceful, and as ingenious as any other capitalist, these ladies of the night developed their own methods of fighting back. Forced for the most part into silent rebellion, they simply relocated straight to where it would hurt the card-carrying reformers the most: into the heart of downtown, right on Main Street in the core of Helena's famous "Last Chance Gulch." In this new, more centralized locale, they proceeded with business as usual, only this time in a more hole-and-corner fashion.

On the right, the Boston Block at 19½ Main Street (now the walking mall on Last Chance Gulch) housed the Boston Clothing Company, which sold "furnishings" on the ground level. During Prohibition, Levy ran her brothel and speakeasy in the upper level. In 1933, she opened the Silver Dollar Bar in the St. Louis Block (left). Another Helena madam, Pearl Maxwell, ran her business in Ida's previous space at the Boston Block until she died in 1953. PHOTOGRAPH COURTESY OF SUSAN BAZAAR.

Records indicate that, within six years of her arrival in Helena, Ida was residing at the International Hotel on Main Street—roughly where the Lewis & Clark County Library and Pioneer Park are located today—running a brothel on the second and third floors, paying rent to the Lissner family, who owned the building itself. Montana attorney general-elect S. C. Ford declared he would strictly enforce the provisions of state law making it a misdemeanor for any property owner to permit a building to be used as a house of ill fame. In other words, property owners would be prosecuted before the tenants running the brothels would. Although Ida was required to appear in court for operating her business in the International Hotel, she managed to keep her doors open. Apparently, the state did not have sufficient evidence to prosecute Ida or the landlords. Then, in 1919, after the enactment of Prohibition across the state and soon the nation, she relocated a few blocks down the street to the upper levels of a building called the Boston Block, which housed a clothing company on the ground level. While in the Boston Block premises, Ida had at least three run-ins with the law, once in 1921, then in 1925, and once more in 1930—each time for running a speakeasy out of a back room in her brothel, rather than for prostitution. As was typical in the day, women of the night trade were frequently indicted for selling alcohol while other community members were overlooked for doing the same. Despite occasional encounters with the law, however, Ida managed to stay out of jail as well as keep her Helena operation up and running all the way through to the end of Prohibition and into the mid-1950s.

In 1933, Ida Levy went legit with the liquor. She moved her business into the building next door, the St. Louis Block, where she ran a fully stocked watering hole on the ground floor, called the Silver Dollar Bar. As far as her family back East knew, she was a reputable bar owner, and that was the extent of it. Anyone who had cared to look more closely would have quickly realized that it must have been an improbably booming bar business to support the lifestyle she enjoyed. According to Ida's grandneice, Susan Bazaar, Ida would head back to New York on occasion, usually over the holidays, and would take her nieces and nephews on shopping sprees to the finest downtown retailers, buying anything they wanted, barring no expense.

"Ida would take us to Radio City Music Hall and to Lindy's Deli in Manhattan for cheesecake," said Bazaar. "When she was unable to visit us over the holidays, she would send lavish gifts from the finest New York City department stores." Little did they know that the main source of her wealth was services offered in the upper suites of the Silver Dollar Bar, known as Ida's Rooms, an enterprise she successfully operated in that location for more than twenty years. According to Bazaar, the family didn't know about Ida's nefarious career until the

1970s, after the madam had died. "My mother met somebody while traveling, who knew Ida and told her," she said. "We laughed."

Ida also had a son, Murray Hirsch, whom Bazaar was unaware of until one of her cousins told her about him. Murray died in a car wreck in April 1925, when he was just twenty-one. At the time he lived in Passaic, New Jersey, but had traveled out of town to watch his high school alma mater play the boys' scholastic basketball tournament in Glens Falls, New York, which would determine the champions of New York, New Jersey, and New England. The boys of Passaic High—known fondly as "the wonderteam" after being undefeated for 159 games over the course of nearly seven years—had just crushed the boys of Lenox, Massachussetts, 75 to 11.

Murray was traveling back home with three other friends, his buddy Max Schiffman at the wheel. As the blithesome four cruised along the west bank of the Hudson River, Max stepped on the gas to pass a Cadillac loaded with other fans from Passaic. They very likely could have been having a jovial shouting match with the other car's passengers as they sped by, and Max likely got distracted, causing his car to careen out of control, off the road, and into a ditch. All four passengers were ejected in four different directions, with Max landing in a tree.

According to an article in the *Helena Independent Record,* a telephone lineman who happened to be working at the time witnessed the accident and cut into a wire to telephone for help. Once help arrived, Murray picked himself up and walked over for assistance, but he collapsed as rescue workers guided him into the ambulance. His liver had been punctured, and he died from internal injuries a couple of hours later. His three friends all survived.

Ida had likely just missed the window of opportunity to see her son before he died; she, herself, had been en route to Passaic, New Jersey, to visit her ailing mother when she got news of the accident.

Ida's career spanned both world wars. Soon after the country got involved in World War II, the army chose Fort William H. Harrison, just three miles west of Helena, as the training grounds for what became the famous Devil's Brigade, an elite American-Canadian commando unit. Officers and enlisted men endured rigorous training in the harsh elements of a Montana winter, snowshoeing, mountain climbing, and

Ida Levy was respected by many in Helena, in part for her charitable donations toward community causes. PHOTOGRAPH COURTESY OF SUSAN BAZAAR.

skydiving to prepare for combat in the unforgiving mountains of Italy and southern France. To unwind over the weekends, the soldiers spent their time relaxing in Helena at the most popular brothel in town, cozying up to the women in the upstairs quarters of Ida's establishment. The ladies in Ida's house warmed up to the boys so much that at least one wedding came out of the connection between them. Even Ida herself was known to send letters to some of the boys when they headed out to fight overseas.

Helena's distinguished madam was well loved, not only by those visiting her rooms, but by others around the community. Every Christmas, she would throw an extravagant buffet party for all the people who made deliveries or did odd jobs for her. She tipped very generously. She had a big heart and a propensity for quiet philanthropy, anonymously donating to local charities and community organizations on a regular basis. For example, she once secretly gave $10,000 to fund the municipal swimming pool. She commanded such community respect, in fact, that she seemed to forget that not all viewed her profession so benignly. To her credit, she never let such views prevent her from conducting herself as anything less than the pillar of the community that she was.

In one episode from 1947, for example, Ida attempted to enter a meeting held down in Butte for the Business and Professional Women's Club. The gentleman greeting her at the door informed her she was not welcome because the event was for "professional women, not whores." Perturbed, but undaunted, Ida spontaneously snapped back, "But Robbie, I'm the most professional woman here!"

First and foremost, Ida Levy was a prudent businesswoman. She possessed a quick and vivid wit, which, along with her shrewd public relations strategies, charmed her customers and the community at large. Once she was called to federal court as a government witness to testify about a Choteau man accused of selling her five gallons of booze without having the proper license. Ida testified that the alcohol had merely been provided for a party. When the prosecutor scoffed at the need for five whole gallons of alcohol for one party, Ida simply shrugged and declared, "Well, it was a big party."

Perhaps the most fitting and memorable monument to the legacy of Ida Levy would have been that New Year's Ball at the Civic Center— an occasion nearly as ephemeral as the bloom of the lilacs in Helena's spring. And yet for a few hours one winter night, the ballroom was a waltz of distinguished men who no doubt had indulged themselves throughout the year in discussions of law, policy, and business

Ida—Just an Old Family Friend

Harry Barnett, a native of Helena who is a retired entertainment lawyer now residing in Georgia, knew Ida Levy very well. She was an old family friend.

"There were only about ten Jewish people living in Helena at the time," he said. "We were in the same tribe." When Harry was a young teen, he would help Ida fill out forms at the train depot, since she couldn't read or write in English—only in Yiddish.

His father had rented a storefront from the madam at 21 South Main, next door to Ida's Silver Dollar, and Harry felt right at home among Helena's matrons. On the other side of Ida's place was The Dell, a parlor she also owned, but Dorothy Baker was managing it at the time. On the other side of that was Pearl Maxwell's Royal Rooms.

When his mother fell sick, Ida would come to his house and cook for him and his brother, Norman. "She was a fantastic cook," reminisced Harry. "It was typical Jewish food. . . . She would always close down her business on Jewish holidays to cook." He often would pack his car full of his school buddies to go pick up a meal, parking at Ida's back entryway, then running out, sharing spurious tales with his envious cohorts about his run-ins with Ida's ladies.

Harry reflects on Ida's generosity very fondly. One Saturday evening stands out in his mind in particular. When he was sixteen, he dressed up in a topcoat, intent on finding a bar that would serve him drinks. His sick mother was returning the next day from San Francisco after having had a major operation. While he was seated at a bar, a juvenile officer came up behind him and inquired about Harry's age. Needless to say, the boy was carted off to jail, at what is now the Myrna Loy Center for the Performing Arts. "My mother was coming home the next day, and I couldn't talk them out of it," said Harry. The woman who had been taking care of Harry and his brother called Ida, who placed a call with her lawyer friend, Wellington Rankin. According to Harry, Rankin immediately got on the horn to the jailhouse, which resulted in a shouting match between Rankin and the attending officers.

Harry got home in time to greet his mother at the door.

enterprises at Ida's Silver Dollar Bar, flushed on whiskey and the foot rubs of Ida's upstairs ladies, and now here those men were, known to one another by the swatch of yellow wrapped about their necks, infused with the passionate fragrance of Helena's most prominent springtime flower. Surely they all must have smiled at one another in humbled recognition, bemused by the odor of lilacs and Ida Levy's subtle reminder of how thin is the veneer between propriety and salacity.

Big Dorothy—The Fix Was In

After entering the back gate at 1 P.M. on April 17, 1973, city officials climbed the steps to the back door of 19½ Main Street. They were armed with a court order for the abatement of Dorothy's Rooms, Helena's notorious and last working brothel, and they intended to shut down the house once and for all. Once inside, they found themselves in a small kitchen. To the casual observer, it looked like an ordinary kitchen in an ordinary house. A coffee pot sat warm on the counter, its little red light still glowing. Across from the built-in range and dishwasher was a nondescript cabinet. On top of it sat a small statue with a message that seemed particularly apropos to the occasion: "It's a beautiful day . . . now watch some bastard louse it up."

Beyond the kitchen, the men passed through a long series of hallways that led to several dimly lit lounges and bedrooms. Long curtains hung from the windows. There were seven bedrooms in all, each flaunting a different color scheme for its velvet bedspread, matching furniture, and plush carpet. Beyond these quarters, the officers entered the private chambers of the proprietress, where they found an ailing Dorothy Josephine Baker, a 240-pound diabetic who had clearly seen better days. She was into her fourth week of having a terrible flu and looked emotionally "beaten down," according to one reporter who had accompanied the city officials. Another less-than-favorable account described her as "dumpy." Despite her failing health, the men escorted the feeble, fifty-seven-year-old madam out of the building. She was wearing a simple housedress and left with nothing more than the coat on her back and the Coke-bottle glasses on her face. All of her other possessions remained inside. Escorted out with her was one of Dorothy's employees, Diane Rogers—known by her clients as Dariana Judge Dion—who had been hiding in a closet when police initially arrived. (The only other person in the house at the time, a maid, was allowed to leave on her own.) A fleet of paddy wagons waited for the two women on Main Street, which in 1973 extended beyond Sixth Avenue and Broadway and was Helena's main downtown thoroughfare. Not long after the abatement proceeding, that stretch of Main was renamed Last Chance Gulch and converted to a walking mall as part of Helena's contentious plan for urban renewal.

The scene seemed a little much to thirty-year-old Pete Lenmark, a city planner at the time, as he gazed down from a second-story window across the street. A crowd of police and sheriff vehicles surrounded Big Dorothy's place.

"It was excessive," he said. It had been a cool spring day in Helena with overcast skies. Big Dorothy and Diane Rogers shivered outside when workmen approached the building with fresh sheets of plywood straight from the lumberyard and boarded up all the windows. "I was overwhelmed," Lenmark added. "She had on a dress like my grandmother would wear. And they locked her out of her home, just like that. She wasn't able to get her personal stuff out. There was no cease and desist."

Pete Lenmark realized he was witnessing the end of an era that was significant for Helena.

At the time, Lenmark worked in the City Hall Annex in the Dunphy Block, which housed the Model Cities Office, City Engineer Office, Director of Public Works and Planning Office, and Urban Renewal. Helena's downtown had been undergoing a transformation over the last few years after being selected with Butte and other cities around the state to participate in the federal Model Cities program, implemented seven years prior. The program gave cities access to federal funding for improving their communities. While it seemed a good idea at the time, given the dilapidated status of much of Helena's downtown, many of its residents came to view the move toward urban renewal as a misguided effort that erased entire swaths of Helena's early history as the wrecking balls destroyed some of the city's most famous and best-loved buildings. One critic recently described urban renewal in Butte as "cultural and architectural thalidomide," an apt phrase that captures the failure of its good intentions.

It was true that Helena's downtown core at the time was literally falling apart. Absentee ownership was a considerable problem, with most businesses failing and about eighty percent of the buildings in the south part of downtown unable to meet building codes. Nevertheless, the razing of more than 240 buildings in Helena's historic district came as a crushing blow to those citizens who had a warm affection for Helena's unique, historic charm. To those who cared about historic preservation, urban renewal replaced one form of blight with another, and in doing so removed all possibility of rehabilitating those irreplaceable period structures. On the former Wall Street alone (which connected Last Chance Gulch to Park), three modern buildings and a park replaced 150 original structures. Included in the demolition was West State Street and what remained of old Chinatown, destroying almost completely any trace of the history of Helena's original prostitution district. All in all, only about seventeen of Helena's historic buildings, those in Reeder's Alley included, and eighteen façade easements withstood the drastic makeover. According to one account in the *Independent Record*, "the well beaten path up the alley [behind Dorothy's Rooms] was blocked by wrecking crews. Historic landmarks were razed on both sides of the Gulch." Buildings dropped all around, and Dorothy's building, the St. Louis Block, was one of the original few miraculously left standing.

Ironically, Big Dorothy had been one of the lone entrepreneurs voluntarily taking initiative with urban renewal to improve the community. City commissioners awarded her a $500 grant, which she sunk into a months-long remodel of the ground floor. She intended to use that floor as a retail space for a legitimate business. Construction was still underway, with arrangements in place for tenants to occupy the refurbished space, when she was given the final boot.

"What the hell?" spouted a frustrated Don Kerns to a reporter for the *Independent Record*. He was Helena's community development director at the time, who likely also witnessed the whole scene from the City Hall Annex across the street. "She's the one person trying her best to bring her property up to city codes."

But the issue was more complicated. City commissioners got a lot of flak for handing Big Dorothy federal money to renovate. For starters, urban renewal regulations forbade the city from dealing with illegal businesses. Community members had been following the soap-opera-like tale in the local papers. Letters flooded into the *Independent Record* in response to the coverage. Some argued that Dorothy was an institution in the business community and should have been allowed to continue her business and efforts to better the city.

Others argued she had no right to the funds because she ran an illicit business. Before the final abatement, one city commissioner had been demanding an investigation of Big Dorothy, and the debate at a city commission meeting flared into an uproar. Mayor Stephen F. Keim was fed up with the hullabaloo. "I'm getting a headache on this," he proclaimed. At one meeting, he dumped a stack of fan mail before the commissioners and said, "Everybody knows what business is in Dorothy's Rooms."

County attorney Thomas Dowling tried to placate community members who were irate about Big Dorothy receiving the grant. "If Dorothy is operating an illegal business, and if I can get a witness to testify to that effect, I can bring her to court.... Without a complaint or a witness, I have no indication that she is doing anything illegal," he said. "I'd like nothing better than to close her down if she's running an illegal business."

Dowling finally got his wish. He sent two undercover investigators to visit Dorothy's Rooms. One was able to testify that Dorothy had, indeed, sold him drinks without a valid liquor license. As well, the investigator paid $20 to observe a woman squirming around, naked, on the bed. Dowling had what he needed for his final injunction against Dorothy Josephine Baker.

Once Dorothy's door were officially shuttered, even more letters flooded the papers.

I wonder if the persons responsible for closing down Dorothy Baker's and putting her out of her home realize how much business that her and others like her have given to this town.

I used to work at the New York store, a shoe store, and later was part owner of Henessy's Grocery. I have seen the hundreds of dollars that these women have spent in just these places of business alone.

Also, would the people who closed her down take on the responsibility of donating to the charity functions that these women have donated to over the years?

Another wrote in:

Dorothy ran her place for a number of years and the list of her patrons would make the who's who column look small. I say to all you Helena hypocrites, you lost your best tourist attraction and a true asset to the town.

And yet another:

Bank presidents, doctors, lawyers, politicians, respected family men and even men of the cloth were clients of Dorothy's. All I know is that I cannot think of one instance where a man was riled or taken advantage of, or had his arm twisted to visit her emporium.

This was not the first time Dorothy's Rooms—a not-so-discreet-but-oh-so-legally-elusive house of disrepute—was faced with the threat of closure, but it was the first—and last—abatement the proprietress would face. With the windows of the premises now boarded up because she had been running a house "for the purpose of lewdness, assignation, and prostitution," Big Dorothy would never again see the inside of her home, which had been a veritable economic institution in Helena for nearly twenty years.

The madam had withstood three previous raids throughout her career by simply ignoring the charges put against her and carrying on with business as usual, running her high-class bordello without a hitch, at least for the most part. According to an essay by Helena historian Ellen Baumler, "Dorothy's Rooms: Helena's Last, and Some

Say Best, Place," Dorothy's house was "quiet and orderly . . . clean as a kernel of corn." (One man, divulging that he had visited Dorothy's place to ostensibly "fix the plumbing," noticed that the madam had posted health certificates above all of the beds.)

Nor was one likely to find boisterous or lewd roughnecks making trouble in the place. Rather, it was frequented by Helena's most notable suits and ties. If a client did happen to start causing trouble for one of the women, Dorothy would turn on a wall switch in one of the sitting rooms. On the other side of that wall was a small cubby with a window leading outside to the back alley. Mounted to the window was a shelf on which sat a red police-car rotator light, which would flash when the sitting-room switch was flipped, indicating trouble inside. Overall, Big Dorothy's clients minded their manners. She was imposing, and actually, well, *big*. And she wasn't afraid to rely on some of her natural, athletic strength when she found herself backed in a corner.

Before working as Dorothy Josephine Baker in Helena, she grew up as Dorothy "Dodie" Putnam in Great Falls, in a staunch Catholic household. Her 1933 high school yearbook reveals a girl who was socially active as a member of the French club and as student organizer of a school ball. (Next to her senior yearbook photograph, Dodie wrote a cryptic note—"Don't tell"—to classmate Clifford Frank. Coincidentally, the *1934 Roundup* pictures Clifford Frank right next to classmate Virginia E. Flanagan, the future wife of Montana Supreme Court justice John Harrison—the man who worked doggedly as a district attorney to shutter Dorothy's Rooms.) But young Dodie had athletic tendencies to boot, participating in tumbling and track, as well as playing volleyball and basketball. So one can assume Big Dorothy wouldn't hesitate to drop a shoulder into the ribcage of an opponent or two.

As an adult, she reportedly intimidated even officers of the law. During one midnight raid, she got into a scuffle with the chief criminal deputy as he tried to drag out one of her employees, who happened to be tending bar without a liquor license, considered a felony at the time. The deputy prevailed, but the encounter left an impression on him, and he declared, "She's a strong woman!"

Big Dorothy's real name was Dorothy "Dodie" Putnam, pictured here in her high school yearbook, the 1933 Roundup. PHOTOGRAPH COURTESY OF MONTANA HISTORICAL SOCIETY RESEARCH CENTER, Z371.8976.

Perhaps one of her longtime nemeses put it most succinctly. Judge John C. Harrison spent a good portion of his career working to shut down Dorothy's operation. "I would've hated like hell to have met her in a dark alley," he said.

After establishing himself as a hard-hitting attorney, John C. Harrison went on to serve on the Montana Supreme Court from 1961 to 1995. PHOTOGRAPH COURTESY OF THE STATE LAW LIBRARY OF MONTANA.

Judge Harrison had his first face-off with Dorothy when he was a local county attorney and was just beginning to realize what an enormous feat he was undertaking when he started proceedings to close her house down. The business of prostitution was much bigger and more complicated than he had anticipated.

To take one example, a local doctor had reported to the health department that Dorothy's Rooms were a vector of venereal disease. The health department was required to report it to the county attorney and ask for action, so Harrison filed an injunction against Dorothy. According to Harrison, it "created one of the great hornet's nests of the year in that office." He received a string of calls from prominent businessmen and professionals asking him "what the hell" he was doing to one of the best businesses on Main Street. Two district judges called him in for a meeting. "They were astounded at my judgment and went so far as to infer I was stupid," recalled Harrison.

In preparing for court, he made arrangements with the local sheriff to park in the alley behind Dorothy's Rooms and snap photos of the departing guests. Helena was a small town, and Dorothy was an institution in that small town. She was even on a first-name basis with the local papers. Harrison wanted to have some idea of who visited the place, so he wouldn't end up with any of them on the jury. Over a month's time, they had collected a startling collection of familiar faces, one of whom was a bachelor friend of Harrison's—a judge from out of town who occasionally came to Helena to preside over litigation when a local judge was disqualified from a case.

"I knew the fix was in," professed Harrison.

When the case came to trial, the young county attorney called forth his star witness, the doctor who originally reported the venereal disease, thinking he had an easy win. After about five minutes of testimony, the presiding judge interrupted and asked the purpose of the testimony. Harrison had done his homework and cited two Montana cases setting precedence for that type of witness. "That may well be the law in Montana," the judge put forth, "but this is Lewis and Clark County." The evidence was not allowed, and Harrison saw his case "slipping out the window."

During a recess, Harrison contacted a twenty-five-year-old man from Lincoln who had visited Dorothy's rooms on occasion and was, at the last minute, willing to testify. Harrison had until 2 P.M. to get the witness into court, so he sent the deputy sheriff off to pick the man up. With five minutes to spare, the sheriff raced back in with the witness. They entered a hushed courtroom. "You could whisper, and it would have sounded like a cannon," said Harrison.

Seated in the witness stand, Harrison's friend gave an account of his experience in Dorothy's place. He testified that the clients were required to buy a drink prior to seeing the girls. Then, while maintaining unwavering eye contact with Dorothy's hotshot defense lawyer, Wellington Rankin (who Harrison claimed was known to pull some ethically questionable maneuvers in the courtroom), he continued to explain how he paid a beauty with a French accent $25 to have sex, and they completed the act.

The astounded Rankin opted out of a cross-examination. Harrison and the sheriff took their friend out for a victory steak dinner that night, without realizing their celebration was a bit premature.

The next day in court, it was actually the liquor sale that stuck. The witness had testified to paying for every shot glass of booze, proving Dorothy had violated state law for selling without a license, which was a serious offense. She was slapped with a felony charge and faced a possible yearlong sentence. She pled guilty, and the judge charged her only a $500 fine. As if to rub salt in the wound, Wellington Rankin agreed to have his client pay the fine.

"By that time, I knew I was being had," said Harrison. He immediately stood up, Montana Code book in hand, and offered to give the presiding judge a closer look at the statute, which required a minimum $1,000 fine. "There was considerable consternation, to say the least," Harrison added. Wellington had to go get another $500 from his client.

The third day in court was devoted to arguments on Dorothy's abatement. An order to close her doors was drawn and served. But on the following day, everyone was called in to court again to learn someone had tampered with the order the judge had signed, requiring a retrial. The judge disqualified himself from the case and called in another judge to preside over the retrial. After reading the testimony, the new judge recused himself from the case as well.

Finally, a new district court judge from out of town swooped in to oversee the trial to its end. And Harrison's initial hunch was right on the mark. The fix *was* in.

The new presiding judge was none other than the free-living bachelor whose mug could be seen in the stack of photos of all the visitors leaving Dorothy's famous back door that was sitting on the desk back in Harrison's office.

It wasn't until he was serving as supreme court justice that Harrison finally witnessed the final closing of Big Dorothy's business in April 1973. Most Helena longtimers figured Big Dorothy would open her doors again once her trial was over. But less than a month after she was dragged out of her home in handcuffs, she was admitted to a hospital in Great Falls. Ten hours later, on May 14, she died from "acute illness" just a week before she was to plead her case in court.

Dorothy Josephine Baker was well loved by the Helena community, and especially well remembered for her generosity. She was particularly generous to her niece and nephew and had spent a lot of time with them when they were growing up.

"She was a wonderful person," said her niece, Mary Buckley, in a 2012 interview for the *Independent Record.* "I'd go to see her and I'd say, 'That's a beautiful bedspread.' She'd fold it up and give it to me." Buckley had nothing but fond memories of her aunt. "She really loved her family. She had a warm place for all of us. She was a very, very good person. The people of Helena really liked her."

Dorothy paid for her niece and nephew's college education, but her generosity reached beyond her close family circle. In fact, she paid for many aspiring students to attend college without the expectation of reimbursement and with several of them never knowing their benefactor. She was known to lavishly tip the paperboys who delivered to her door. If a local student knocked on her door to sell a box of candy for a fundraiser, Dorothy, dependable customer that she was, often bought the child's entire supply. She bought piles of children's books to donate to local children's homes. Countless charities around town benefited from her unstinting contributions.

City commissioner Ed Loranz was perhaps one of Dorothy's most outspoken admirers. "I've known Dorothy a long time, and she's always been a fine woman. She was always doing something for somebody. She'd lend you money. She'd tip the police off to drug pushers," he said. "Dorothy has just as much right to be part of this town as the air we breathe."

Some air, however, is better cause for bated breath and whispering humbleness. Dorothy's life had thorns hidden among the rosy public

Big Dorothy's longtime lover was James "Toppo" Bittrick, an amateur boxer from Anaconda. PHOTOGRAPH COURTESY OF MONTANA HISTORICAL SOCIETY RESEARCH CENTER, RS 111.

accolades. In particular, she had a soft spot in her heart for a dark-haired, blue-eyed Croatian hunk named James "Toppo" Bittrick. A dead ringer for Cary Grant, he was an amateur middleweight boxer hailing from Anaconda. It's quite possible they had a common-law marriage, because, according to FBI files, he also went by James Baker and Jimmy Baker. Conversely, Big Dorothy appeared as Dorothy Bittrick at various card games reported in the social pages of the Helena paper.

Toppo was a hard hitter, not only in the boxing ring, but in the drug ring as well. According to district attorney records, he had needle marks up and down the insides of his forearms from a $1,000-per-month narcotics habit that Dodie had financially supported for years. In palling around with renowned burglars, addicts, gamblers, and prostitutes, Toppo had been "in and out of every jail on the west coast" on charges of assault, white slavery, theft, and minor offenses—you name it, he did time for it. And oftentimes, Dodie was there to help bail him out.

But, as are most people, Dorothy was a complex character. Madams had to do their fair share of finagling to remain favorable in the eyes of friends, clients, community members, and city officials. It was no easy task, and sometimes their efforts backfired. Despite her generosity toward community members and close personal friends, not everyone spoke favorably of the madam. Supreme court justice John Harrison stuck to the rule of law, sidestepping any attempts by Helena's courtesans to persuade him to look the other way. He could attest to the darker side of Dodie, the side that most of Helena's citizens were unaware of or chose to ignore.

"She was a big, tough bitch," Judge Harrison contended. Throughout his years as county attorney, in all of his dealings with the madam while trying to shut down her house, he was one of the few individuals who had access to Dorothy's confidential FBI records. He recounted that the madam was often strung out on morphine, as was common for many prostitutes. Folks who praised her for ratting out pushers to the police were probably unaware, according to Harrison, that she pushed her own fair share of dope. "It's all in her record."

Big Dorothy's mug shot appeared in a report by the Federal Bureau of Investigation that circulated at a 1962 Montana law enforcement convention. PHOTOGRAPH COURTESY OF MONTANA HISTORICAL SOCIETY RESEARCH CENTER, RS 111.

According to one anonymous letter to the editor that appeared in the *Independent Record* after Dorothy had died, it was the poised Ida Levy who should be remembered favorably by the community, and not the frumpish Big Dorothy.

"Dorothy Baker became infamously known by reason of adverse publicity only," the writer announced. "[Her] predecessor in business, Ida Levy, occupied the same premises for many years before she retired and sold out to Dorothy Baker. Ida conducted herself so as to never draw criticism to herself or her girls. She was never seen in public shabbily dressed. She always dressed well and conducted herself in a manner which never embarrassed any of her many friends of the political or business world who may have called at her premises. . . . Ida Levy was truly better known throughout the state by reason of the warmth of the personal relationships."

3

Butte

A Corrupt and Wide Open Town

"Heathen godless—hell's delight,
Rude by day and lewd by night,
Dwarfed by man, enlarged by brute,
Ruled by roué and prostitute,
Purple robed and pauper clad
Raving, rotting, money-mad,
Squirming herd in Mammon's mesh,
Wilderness of human flesh.
Crazed by Avarice, Lust, and Rum,
Butte, thy name is Delerium."

—WARREN DAVENPORT, FROM *BUTTE AND*
MONTANA BENEATH THE X-RAY (1908)

Butte, Montana—the name alone is enough to conjure the entire
panorama of the Gilded Age West, when muddy alleys skirting

crude shacks and log cabins seemed to transform overnight into tow-ering brick buildings and glassed storefronts with the latest fashions from New York and Chicago. Though it is a modest western town of 30,000 residents today, known mainly for its Superfund sites (includ-ing the infamous Berkeley Pit), there was a time not so long ago when Butte was a cosmopolitan metropolis, the biggest city between Seattle and Minneapolis.

Unlike a lot of boomtowns in the West whose fortunes faded into sagebrush and memory as the gold petered out, Butte became an enduring mining center, an extensive industrial park of headframes, concentrators, and smelters marching through town down to the flats below. In the century between 1875, when Bill Farlin sank the first shaft in the Travona mine, leading to a rich lode of silver ore, and 1980, when the Anaconda copper smelter finally called it quits, his-torians estimate that more than $30 billion was extracted from the nondescript hillside on the flanks of the Continental Divide called "The Butte Hill."

At its peak, Butte far surpassed Helena and Great Falls for the fame of its nightlife. The entire country knew that Butte was "a wide open town," which meant a person could satisfy just about any vice on its streets. The only other urban centers in the country with red light districts as notorious as Butte were New Orleans, San Francisco, and Chicago, and when the last Barbary Coast district brothels shuttered in 1917, Butte replaced San Francisco as having the largest red light district in the nation.

Between the scores of men trying to wrest a living from the mines and the executives and capitalists who filled boardrooms and clubs and had the desire and wealth to indulge themselves however they wished, prostitution naturally flourished in Butte. According to *Copper Camp*, a book sponsored by the Works Projects Administration, "a favorite bawdyhouse ballad of early-day Western mining camps went: 'First came the miners to work in the mine, then came the ladies who lived on the line.'" And as historian Derek Strahn puts it, madams in Butte distinguished themselves as especially powerful and legend-ary: "Ambitious, assertive, and uncommonly nonconformist, these strong-willed madams took no prisoners in their attempts to change

In its heyday, Butte's nightlife rivaled any American city of the times. In this street scene from 1939, nattily dressed men enjoy an evening at the Board of Trade.

social conventions and, thereby, define a strikingly non-traditional life for themselves."

The hurdy-gurdy houses arose in Butte as early as 1878, but by 1884, the well-known "line" was established, first called "Pleasant Alley," a moniker replaced a half century later by the more enticing "Venus Alley." The geography of the red light district followed a southerly trajectory, beginning in the late 1870s high up the hill on Park Street, its focus eventually shifting a block down the hill to Galena Street, and finally expanding to include the especially high-class establishments on Mercury Street yet another block south in uptown Butte.

In his lyrical homage to Montana, *Montana: High, Wide, and Handsome*, Joseph Kinsey Howard devoted a few pages to the "sporting people" of Butte, which was the term the girls used to refer to themselves in the 1940s when Howard spoke to them. "After we go out of the alley, we're just like anybody else," one girl related to him. "We work for our money; in good times the take'll run to $100 a week for some of the younger and prettier ones." Howard marveled that the "restricted district" of Venus Alley by 1943 was "just two-and-a-half blocks from Butte's new modern high school," but attributed the atypical arrangement as typical of Butte, a town that took a pragmatic and inclusive approach to its women of the red light district. As his unnamed source confided, "Butte figures we give value for the money and we're just as good as anybody, so we can live in nice places and it don't matter where we eat . . . they don't kick us out of restaurants or make it tough for us, like some places I've been. . . ."

Two of the earliest prostitutes in Butte turned out to be among the longest-serving, though it is unclear whether they ever operated as actual madams. Both "Carmen" and "Nigger Liz," as they were infamously known, plied their trade until, as one source recounts, "they were withered, toothless hags." An old-timer in Butte was reported to have observed that "if the wages of sin are death, those two old girls had a hell of a long wait for payday."

A "conservative estimate," according to *Copper Camp*, was that between 1904 and 1917, "there were close to a thousand girls quartered in the district." Such a significant workforce demanded supervision, and many of the houses became known by the madams who ran them. Interestingly, while the finest establishments were owned and run by women, the poorer quality premises in Butte tended to be owned and financed by wealthy, prominent, and "respectable" men who capitalized on the demand for prostitution. In an essay called "Devil's Perch," historian and leading authority on the history of Montana prostitution Ellen Baumler notes the prevalence of a blatant double-standard in Butte: while paragons of virtue such as Anton Holter and Lee Mantle owned some of the worst cribs in the district, they were insulated from charges of vice or impropriety. Holter, who lived in Helena, benefitted from his distance from the scene—it relieved him of having to "explain." As for Mantle, as Baumler puts it, knowledge of his association with red light activity "did not affect his popularity, for Butte and Montana always held him in high regard." Naturally, the women working in the premises they owned did not enjoy such "high regard," nor were their living circumstances nearly as comfortable. The disparity was ameliorated only slightly by the fact that the best houses, only one street over from those owned by men, were governed by powerful madams.

In fact, some of the West's most famous madams called Butte, Montana, home. The rolls of well-known Butte madams include such characters as Ruby Garrett, for example, "Montana's last madam," who died in 2012 at age ninety-four, having been proprietor of the Dumas Hotel, the very last openly operated brothel in Montana, which closed its doors in 1982. There was also Lou Harpell, famous proprietor of the Hotel Victoria at 11 East Mercury, one of the finest of the fine houses, whose girls were known the country over as "the most beautiful women in the world," a sobriquet that originated with Earl Carroll, the well-known American theatrical producer of the early twentieth century, but more famously echoed by Charlie Chaplin after a visit to Butte. (Chaplin also added that in Butte, "if one saw a pretty girl smartly dressed, one could rest assured she was from the red light quarter, doing her shopping.") Bertha Leslie was memorable as the manager of the hotel just next door to the Hotel Victoria, the Windsor Hotel at 9 East Mercury, a deluxe establishment with fancy furnishings such as "satin-covered sofas and chairs, gilt-framed mirrors, tapestries, and plants in brass jardinières," according to one source. Nearly contemporary with Ruby Garrett, Beverly Snodgrass famously operated a couple of houses in Butte in the 1960s, one on Wyoming Street and the other on Mercury, an enterprise that gathered headlines when Ms. Snodgrass revealed in an investigation the exorbitant fees to city officials she had been forced to pay in order to conduct her illicit business. Perhaps most famous of all was madam Mae Malloy, who has gone down in history as the brothel owner who was among the very few to withstand an invasion from temperance crusader Carrie Nation. As one writer put it, Carrie Nation may have won the temperance war, "but she lost the battle for Butte."

More than any other city in Montana, prostitution and the lives of the madams and the social scene were intimately connected—"intertwined," as Ellen Baumler puts it. Montana madams were fundamentally businesswomen who operated in almost every way in accordance with the codes—both social and moral—of their times, with the exception of the actual product they provided. Yet even the sale of sex in Butte, while it may not have pleased the moralists on every corner, was perceived by authorities and the madams themselves

A courtesan of Butte's Venus Alley strikes a "come hither" pose in a decidedly industrial tableau. PHOTOGRAPH COURTESY OF THE BUTTE-SILVERBOW PUBLIC ARCHIVES, PH373.

as a sort of necessary evil—not unlike hardrock mining itself, which brutalized men and destroyed the landscape. The horrors men faced thousands of feet underground, including the constant fear of a cave-in and the more protracted fear of eventually succumbing to silicosis, were certainly matched by their counterparts in the cribs to the north of Mercury Street where the lower-class brothels and prostitutes worked in abysmal conditions. If "the Con" (short for consumption) was the inevitable prospect facing many miners, then alcoholism, drug addiction, or violence was often the inevitable end for the prostitutes of Venus Alley.

The "Richest Hill on Earth" left even many of the women in the finer houses spiraling into debt, with little chance for escape. A madam's house was, essentially, the company store—providing money for the required fancy clothes and everyday living costs for its employees, who in turn had to pay double the price they would for the same goods elsewhere. Employees had to remain loyal to their sponsoring matrons or risk losing everything they had and finding themselves on the streets. And Montana's scabrous reputation marked even its elite women of the night trade, rendering them unmarketable in the established houses back East.

Madams were not unlike the mine owners and employers who profited from the laborers working for them. They, too, tended to enjoy a standing in society quite apart from the average worker. Madams like Ruby Garrett, Beverly Snodgrass, Mae Malloy, and Lou Harpell succeeded in business and made names for themselves against odds stacked unfavorably against women in general, but especially against women in the sex industry. In the same way that history remembers the names of the Copper Kings—Marcus Daly, William A. Clark, and Augustus Heinze—while forgetting the countless names of the miners who labored daily to make their fortunes, so too does the historical record include the names and stories of the madams who helped write the story of Butte, even as the names and faces of the many women who worked Venus Alley are doomed to oblivion.

Lou Harpell—A Big Haul

Lou Harpell was among the most famous of the early Butte madams. The hotel she ran on the north side of Mercury Street bedazzled her clients with its opulence. "It is doubtful if in the city there were any more elaborately furnished residences," wrote an unnamed journalist in *Copper Camp*. These pretentious houses of ill repute were showcases of grandeur and the latest decorative embellishments: silk drapes, the finest brass fixtures (some even of gold), and battalions of Chinese and "colored" servants to greet and serve customers in more mundane ways. Whereas the old Galena Street row houses served a clientele drawn mainly from the miners and the working classes, the establishments on Mercury catered to the very elite, the wealthiest of the mining magnates and the banking industry. And Harpell's reputation among the social elite was such that she dauntlessly advertised her establishments in programs for local theater productions and the horse-racing track.

The madam's roots are elusive, however. According to the 1864 *Butte City Directory*, her name was Mary L. Harpell. The 1900 census, on the other hand, has her name recorded as Loy Harpell, born in 1938 and hailing from Germany. Several writers have loosely connected Lou Harpell to a prominent midwestern madam working under the name of Lou Harper, which would make sense, as women in this line of work tended to move around, changing their names in the process.

The woman named Lou Harper opened an elegant brothel, the Mansion, in Chicago's red light district during the Civil War. She was said to have taken in lonely bluecoats to serve her country, so to speak, but mostly targeted wealthy clientele—business executives, professionals, and lonely lads with loaded wallets. Hers was a classy establishment, devoid of the gaudy trappings that screamed of ill repute—no red light, no large house numerals, no plush red draperies typical of cathouses of the day. Her entryway bore a simple sign that read, "Miss Lou Harper." Men were not admitted if they didn't abide by the house's dress code, or if they exhibited lewd or drunken behavior. She demanded respect for her ladies as well, insisting they all be introduced by name. She also demanded her ladies live up to that respect, requiring they dress in fine gowns, remain free of foul language, and keep clear-headed, staying away from liquor. Harper's was the finest bordello Chicago had to offer—until the fateful night of October 8, 1871.

A fire sparked, purportedly in the barn of Patrick and Catherine O'Leary, a humble couple who had immigrated to America from Ireland. A local newspaper reporter giving an account of the story in the *Chicago Tribune* confessed to fabricating the famous tale about Mrs. O'Leary leaving a lantern lit in the shed, which her cow subsequently kicked over. A more likely account tells of the O'Learys' son James Patrick—who would eventually become the kingpin of Chicago's gambling circuit, "Big Jim"—gambling with some buddies in the family barn late into the evening, when, in a drunken stupor, one of the men inadvertently tipped over a lantern. Whatever the case, the fire quickly flared up and spread out of control.

High winds and severe drought conditions fed the fury that swept through Chicago's central business district, which was mostly constructed of wood. The blaze rapidly escalated into a fire tornado that crossed the river twice and drove the flames farther and higher. Panicked residents fled on foot, along with many leading their horse-drawn carriages, straight into Lake Michigan to escape with their lives and what few possessions they could grab in their rush to safety. Exhausted fire crews fought the conflagration for three days, with the help of much needed rain falling on the second night of the blaze. It finally fizzled out the next day, leaving a town that was barely recognizable.

Once all the damage was assessed, approximately three square miles of the city center were left in cindered rubble, and nearly 100,000 residents were left homeless with 300 dead. In all, 17,450 buildings were destroyed, with damages estimated at $200 million. Included in the damages would have been Harper's Mansion, which had been seated right in the fiery core. Although Chicagoans didn't allow themselves to be totally beaten down, constructing 6,000 temporary structures within a week after the fire, no official record shows any evidence of Lou Harper continuing her residence, let alone her business, in post-fire Chicago.

Little evidence of her existence is apparent on the historical record for more than ten years, if Lou Harper and Lou Harpell were, in fact, the same person. A madam by the name of Lou Harpell was mentioned in a letter to the editor of the *Salt Lake Herald* in 1883. She was apparently running a brothel on Third Street in Ogden and was described as "a quiet, inoffensive person of the class to which she belongs," which seems to parallel comments about Harper in Chicago and the Harpell appearing in Butte some years later. Apparently, three men were reported to have thrown "a lot of sticks and rocks through the parlor windows, greatly endangering the lives of the inmates." Had Lou Harper started afresh after the great fire burned her out of business? Was she eventually run out of Ogden, to head toward a more welcome reception in Butte? It would be a logical connection, although any certainty would require tying up several loose ends.

Lou Harpell arrived in Butte around 1889. She started working on Park Street, but by 1891, she was running the Hotel Victoria at 11 East Mercury and would continue to do so until the end of her career. Her refined reputation gained her special concessions with city officials. In 1903, when police swooped in and rousted a whole throng of Butte's cathouse women, Harpell's tenants were comparatively well taken care of. The distinguished madam arranged for her ladies to post bail from her house, avoiding court appearances altogether and saving them from the disgrace of public exposure.

Harpell's notoriety did have its shortcomings, however. Through the years, the *Anaconda Standard* reported various accounts of nefarious individuals helping themselves to the riches found in her gilded palace. An 1890 account tells of how two men hoisted a ladder to one of Harpell's second-story windows. One of the men climbed up and entered the house to grab a "seal-skin sacque" of goods and toss it out to his partner waiting below. Soon thereafter, however, the two burglars were surprised when one of their "pals" turned out to be a federal Secret Service agent who testified against them in court. (In those days, the Secret Service was under the Department of the Treasury and investigated counterfeiting and fraud.) Another report from 1898 states that one of her employees, Lulu Garnett, had returned to her room to find $600 in diamonds stolen. Harpell's house had been in the path of some robbers who hit a string of houses that week. Fortunately, they were caught, and Garnett got her jewels back.

But perhaps the worst assault on Harpell's possessions occurred in 1893, when a *Standard* headline read, "It Was A Big Haul."

It was, for the day, a very big haul. And a bold one, too. According to Harpell's account, at ten minutes before three in the afternoon, she had carefully stashed any diamonds, jewelry, watches, and cash safely in her bedroom, which was located just one door down from the house's front entryway. She made sure she locked both the front door and the door to her private quarters before heading down to the basement to join the other ladies for dinner.

As she came back up after the meal, she froze in shock at what she saw.

"My God, I'm robbed!" she screamed. Someone had jimmied the lock on the bedroom door, splintering the door and forcing it open. When she peered inside, to her dismay she found the drawers of her standing bureau had been ransacked and her jewelry cases gone. There was no telling how the intruder had entered the house in the first place, but the curtains on the open window fluttered in the breeze, framing the hole through which he had escaped. The cut screen was placed on the floor. In front of the window was an ornate table that normally displayed a collection of china figures. The burglar had meticulously removed the pieces and placed them in a corner, so he could make his getaway without the noise of them tipping over and breaking. With a stash of goods totaling $3,100 (equivalent today to $78,159), the thief pulled himself through the hole in the screen and dropped fifteen feet from the fire escape to make his getaway. Harpell had a hunch that it was the very same man who tried to break into her room from the fire escape just a week before but had been frightened away. No one had been able to identify him. The crime was never solved.

It's difficult to say for certain that madam Lou Harper of Chicago and Lou Harpell from Butte are one and the same. But perhaps one telling clue occurred on January 15, 1895, with one of the deadliest disasters in the Butte Fire Department's history, known as "Fateful Box 72."

Some railroad workers reported smoke coming from Butte's warehouse district, in the Kenyon-Connell warehouse at the corner of Utah Avenue and Iron Street. Shortly after, the Box 72 alarm was sounded. Within minutes, the firefighters of Central Fire Station arrived for what they assumed would be a routine job. What happened next is recounted today on the Butte-Silver Bow city and county website:

> When they reached the scene of the fire, the flames were bursting through the roof of the warehouse. John Flannery, the plug-man of the crew, made the plug at the hydrant near the Montana

Central Passenger Depot as his duty required him to do. The hose cart and hook and ladder continued on until they reached the warehouses. The nozzle end of the hose was handed over to the Pipeman and Driver, Dave Magee, who took his team a few yards further on, where he stopped and proceeded to blanket the horses, as it was apparent the fire would last for some time.

The hook and ladder apparatus was stopped near the northeast corner of the burning building. . . . Chief A. D. Cameron had given the order to turn on the water and was standing at the hose and straightening out the kinks. Assistant Chief Sloan, axe in hand, was trying to make an opening through the corrugated iron on the northwest corner of the building where the fire appeared to be. Close to the door on the north side were Pipemen Ash and Mose, holding the nozzle and waiting for the stream to be turned on. Near them was Pipeman Ed Sloan, ready for any work that was required. Norling and Fifer were at the hook and ladder apparatus ready to get the ladders out. Part-Paid members of the department; Bowman, Brokaw, Burns, Copeland, Deloughery, and Nolan were near the hose wagon.

Little were these men aware that one of the buildings housed a significant amount of dynamite, along with small iron blocks used as skimming tools for the smelter. A massive explosion in the Kenyon-Connell warehouse resonated through the city, with reports of hearing the blast coming from as far as Three Forks, fifty-five miles away. Debris was later found more than four miles from the blast. As droves of people came to the scene to help, a second explosion in the neighboring Butte Hardware Company warehouse added to the mayhem. Shards from the stored iron blocks blew through the air, impaling everything and everyone in their path. One of the few surviving firefighters, assistant chief Jack Flannery, reported a morbid scene, where "[h]uman bodies lay piled two deep," and "the building's metal siding glowed red-hot." In all, thirteen firefighters—nearly the entire department—died that evening, along with forty-four citizens, possibly more.

This very scene could have been a gruesome reminder of a similar disaster, twenty-four years prior, in the great Chicago fire—if, in fact, Lou Harper and Lou Harpell are the same woman. Under an *Anaconda Standard* headline, "Bowed Down in Sorrow: Butte's Streets Filled with the Mournful Evidences of Her Great Grief: Burying the Heroic Dead To-Day," is an account of a relief committee that collected $11,000 to help those afflicted by the fire.

Perhaps revisiting that all-too-familiar grief, Harpell entered the room where donations were being taken and laid $200 on the table. "I wish it could be more," she said.

Lou Harpell reached deeper into her pockets than did many of the wealthy men of Butte.

Mae Malloy and the "Irish World"

Madam Mae Malloy (some sources list the spelling alternatively as "Maloy") was a madam's madam. Though most of her fame rests on her skirmish with Carrie Nation, she was a legend among the denizens of Butte long before that singular moment of hostility in 1910. For starters, Mae Malloy had brazenly changed the name of the renowned Windsor Hotel—previously run by madams Lillie Reid and Bertha Leslie—to a name with a trace of braggadocio: Irish World.

Malloy's humiliation of Carrie Nation reflected more than just the power of a willful madam. As a moment of conflicting moral views coming head to head, it captured the spirit of Butte. Carrie Nation had encountered little resistance to her Women's Christian Temperance Union campaign wherever she went in the rest of the country. She made headlines by marching into saloons and whorehouses and demanding their closure. Often she took with her an axe or hatchet and vandalized the place, chopping gashes in barrels to waste the whiskey, to the plain dismay of those into whose company she had gone manifestly uninvited. Historian Ellen Baumler reports that one saloon in nearby Anaconda had hung a sign behind the bar proclaiming, "All Nations welcome here except Carrie."

But Butte was different from most of the rest of the country. Earlier efforts at reform in Butte had always met resistance. For example, one prostitute in 1901 complained in the *Butte Miner* that "the moralists of the city were getting too fresh!" Madam Mae Malloy responded to

Bible-thumping Carrie Nation failed to intimidate the denizens of Butte and met her match in the person of madam Mae Malloy. BAIN NEWS SERVICE PHOTOGRAPH COURTESY OF THE LIBRARY OF CONGRESS, LC-DIG-GGBAIN-05640.

the latest moralist efforts with similar aplomb. In fact, she became legendary for meeting Carrie Nation's challenge foot first, literally kicking Carrie's ass out of the Irish World, a celebrated gesture that ensured permanent affection for this feisty madam in the annals of Montana history. The spirited madam went even further, according to historian Derek Strahn, who reports that she shouted as she ran Carrie Nation out on the street, "Get out of my place; get out of my place. Here, you policeman, put this woman out of here. I want these females who are raising a disturbance arrested and taken out of my house."

A decade after Carrie Nation's ignominious defeat in Butte, the Women's Christian Temperance Union achieved its paramount goal with passage of the Eighteenth Amendment in 1919, which made prohibition of alcohol

Butte's Venus Alley, shown here in 1939, was at the center of the mining city's skin trade. ARTHUR ROTHSTEIN PHOTOGRAPH COURTESY OF THE LIBRARY OF CONGRESS, LC-USF33- 003093-M1 [P&P].

the law of the land. They had achieved, at least to all appearances, similar success three years earlier on the prostitution front, when Montana officially enacted statewide legislation criminalizing the red light districts. As with Prohibition, merely criminalizing prostitution did little in the long run to stop it, although in 1917 it did have a short-term effect of dramatically reducing the availability of it. As with most legislative attempts to control vice, criminalization simply nurtured the black market. Nevertheless, by the 1920s, especially in Butte, "the Line" was up and running again in full swing.

After 1910, however, the demimonde in Butte began to gradually lose its glamorous status as prominent clientele started to avoid it. The lavish houses with their ornate furnishings and plush carpets gave way to seedier establishments, venues that gave Venus Alley its sordid reputation. As Butte's cadre of high-class sex workers diminished, the small, exclusive houses like the Dumas with its four women in the employ of madam Grace McGinnis, or the nine women in the employ of madam Ruth Clifford at the Irish World, gave way to much larger, more densely populated hotels catering to a lower class of customer. As Baumler notes, "[D]espite the reformer's best efforts, Butte's demi-monde was larger and seedier than ever by 1910." Indeed, the 1910 census for Butte listed 250 women as prostitutes.

The fine houses of Butte's heyday vanished, and by the 1930s, Venus Alley was relegated to a few houses between Galena and Mercury Streets, the entrances restricted by warning signs that bade "men under 21 Keep Out." This state of affairs persisted into the 1940s, prompting Joseph Kinsey Howard's wry observation about the proximity of prostitution to public high schools in Butte.

EMMA ABBIE—A ROMANTIC CAREER

The most publicity Emma Abbie ever received was when her name appeared (as Emma Abbey) in the *Anaconda Standard* in February 1891 to announce that her enshrouded body rested in the front par-lors of her double-brick house on 11 South Wyoming, surrounded with flowers and awaiting her burial the next day. She had contracted a bout of *la grippe* (influenza) the week prior, which promptly devel-oped into a debilitating case of pneumonia. The madam had spent the last few days of her life tying up loose ends, to ensure that her surviv-ing family members—her mother and two sisters, who were clueless of her life in prostitution—were well taken care of when she finally passed from this world. The headline of the article that appeared that Friday morning simply read, "A Romantic Career."

One would hardly call it romantic. And Miss Abbie knew it. She did what she could to keep a low profile, despite her reputation as one of the "best known sporting women in the Rocky Mountain Region." She somehow managed to remain under the radar of public disgrace associated with the women in her profession. In the entire seven years that she resided in Butte, she maintained a clean police record.

Those who knew her agreed that "she was of genial and kind heart-ed disposition and as much given to good works as a woman in her unfortunate situation could be." But her large circle of friends knew little, if anything, about her life prior to Butte. She was born Emma

Hulsworth in New York, to an Episcopalian minister. She was reportedly well educated and "considered in her girlhood days a lady of refinement." She met and married a traveling salesman from Buffalo, much to the chagrin of her parents. The marriage was not a happy one, and he soon deserted her to continue his sales pitch elsewhere. Left to her own devices in difficult circumstances, Emma opted to head west, landing in Denver, Colorado, and then later moving to the lawless frontier town of Ogden, Utah. She never told her parents about the life she was leading.

No one knows the moniker she used when she resided in Ogden or specifically where she worked and lived. But perhaps she cavorted with the likes of Lou Harpell, because they likely would have been there around the same time. Ogden was incorporated as a city in 1851. San Francisco and Salt Lake were the only other two incorporated cities west of the Missouri River at the time. Floods of Mormons came to settle there, but others with less righteous intents gravitated there as well. With the nearby junction of the Union Pacific and the Central Pacific Railroads in 1869, the town became the major hub connecting trade routes north to south and east to west. The town's motto was, "You can't get anywhere without coming to Ogden." Floods of people looking for opportunity streamed there, inevitably leading to its reputation for quartering coarse and unrefined characters. According to one article in the online citizen's journalism website Utah Stories, "A History of Violence: Ogden's 25th Street," a person was certain to find more than their share of "gambling, shootouts, prostitution, liquor, opium dens, and all manner of vices," you name it, in Ogden's original neighborhood of vice, "Electric Alley." A June 1888 article in the *Western Galaxy* stated that the town "has a future almost certain to put in the shade of any of her sister cities; she is likely to become the Chicago en miniature of the Intermountain region." By the time the 1920s rolled around, Chicago's crime boss, Al Capone, was claimed to have said that Ogden's notorious "Two-Bit Street" was too wild even for the likes of him. Even as early as 1885, Miss Emma, perhaps realizing that the small town was spiraling into squalor, had decided to head up north to Butte.

Once she arrived in Montana, she took the name Emma Abbie

to obscure her true identity and settled into the tenderloin district. At some point, she was able to convince local German entrepreneur Adoph Pincus—a Jewish jeweler, pawnbroker, and investor of sorts—to build a two-story brick building specifically for her to run her brothel. City officials stated that Miss Abbie's house gave them the fewest troubles of all those operating in the tenderloin.

Just before she died, she implored those closest to her who knew her real identity to keep it a secret forever. She did not want "to add another gray hair to the head of her poor sorrowing mother, whom she left long ago in the east." Unfortunately, her wish was not carried out. The *Anaconda Standard* reported the contents of her will about a week later, revealing her birth name and connecting it to her surviving family back East. Her mother's entire head of hair likely blanched silvery white when she learned the truth about her daughter.

BEVERLY SNODGRASS—CORRUPTION EXPOSÉ

On a chilly October morning in 1968, after handing over her personal documents to the Internal Revenue Service and giving a detailed, up-close-and-personal interview with journalist John Kuglin of the *Great Falls Tribune*, the infamous Butte madam Beverly Snodgrass loaded her pickup camper with her belongings, her Bible, and all seven of her pet poodles and departed Butte. Her plan? She was headed cross-country to the nation's capital to visit her state senators, Mike Mansfield and Lee Metcalf. But she wasn't going because she had taken a sudden interest in politics. Rather, she was intent on soliciting their help in shutting down Butte's notoriously corrupt sex industry from which she was burned out. Literally.

According to her accounts, she had grown tired of the payoffs, extortions, and severe beatings she took after refusing to cooperate with local officials. The match in the powder barrel came after she resolved to thwart the greased palms of corrupt individuals, turning instead toward the Psalms of the Good Book. This didn't bode well with the functionaries looking to line their pockets, however. In her interview with the *Tribune*, Snodgrass declared that crooked officials were out to ruin her business with a series of fires that had destroyed her property. And she was afraid for her life.

Born Beulah Maxine Snodgrass in Putney, West Virginia, she grew up in a large, religious family. Two of her brothers went on to work in the ministry.

"I was the one in the family who got off on the wrong track," claimed Beverly, who was fondly known by Butte residents as Bev. "My parents never knew."

She moved to Great Falls and worked as a waitress at Tracy's Diner, which still stands today on the "fun-hundred" block of Central Avenue and is notorious for its oleaginous entreés and noodles topped with hard-boiled eggs. In 1958, she married Maurice Cameron, but the marriage was short-lived. They parted ways, and Beverly relocated to Butte in 1961. There she worked at another greasy spoon until she decided she was ready for a better life. She fell into prostitution, working the nightlife of the Windsor Block.

Beverly entered into the business intending to "save enough money to be able to go away for a couple of years." Her boyfriend at the time, Tony Delmo, helped finance Beverly's purchase of her first brothel at 14 South Wyoming Street,

As a madam, Beverly Snodgrass risked her life by exposing the corruption surrounding prostitution in Butte. PHOTOGRAPH COURTESY OF THE BUTTE-SILVER BOW PUBLIC ARCHIVES.

lending her $4,000, interest free, on the promise that she would pay it back in three years.

In dealing with the logistics of how she would be able to run her brothel under the radar of the law, Beverly sought the assistance of then attorney James D. Freebourn, who eventually became a justice of the district court in Butte. According to Beverly's accounts, in these consultations, Freebourn recommended she pay off local officials, so she could run her business without concern for run-ins with the law. Such a recommendation did not seem nefarious, so she complied and was permitted to openly run her cathouse, trouble free. She employed as many as six women at a time in exchange for putative payments to officials, and the success of her business enabled her to purchase a second house from another madam, two blocks down and around the corner, at 9 Mercury Street, at the time called the Windsor Hotel and later the Missoula Rooms. Although shopworn, it was an impressive three-story, thirty-four-room building, decorated with antique furnishings throughout. Beverly had finally found herself seated as the most prominent courtesan of Butte of that time.

Meantime, according to the madam, her relationship with her lawyer friend, Freebourn, flared into a passionate love affair. A confidential report compiled by W. F. Sanders, a private licensed and bonded investigator for the Northwestern Intelligence Service that Beverly hired to corroborate her story, concurred that her story about the love affair checked out.

But she found she'd been roped into a deal with the devil: she couldn't get out of the business because greedy politicians and a profiteering lover wouldn't allow it. Snodgrass claimed they drained her, taking as much as $75,000 in payoffs over the years—as much as $700 a month—and rendering her incapable of making improvements on her property, which was on the verge of collapsing from disrepair. Beverly hired a private detective, W. F. Sanders, whose investigative report stated that James Freebourn took over the operations of her brothels and had his brother, William, make the monthly collection visits to her houses. According to the report, any time Beverly protested the new business arrangement, James threatened to turn her over to the Internal Revenue Service, stating he could "close her up" at any time. She eventually sold the Windsor in June 1964 and finally boarded up her Mercury house after arsonists torched the place in a series of fires in 1968. She insisted it had been the local authorities in Butte who set the fire, and that they had done so in retaliation for her refusal to pay for enough protection.

But Hell hath no fury like a madam burned, and Beverly Snodgrass hired a detective to expose the corruption she deplored. The detective obliged her with a thorough report that contained many passages making things hot for the police. "Many believe prostitution in Butte is controlled by some national syndicate," wrote the detective, "[but] the syndicate is made up purely of local individuals, most of them so-called officials."

Upon her arrival in Washington, D.C., Snodgrass was able to convince Senator Mansfield to initiate a federal investigation of Butte authorities for any wrongdoing. Even though the case generally fell out of federal jurisdiction, Mansfield asked federal agencies to look into any possible federal violations. Meanwhile, on the local front, Butte Mayor Tom Powers scandalized the rest of the state by claiming, "The people of Butte want prostitution," and at least "we're honest in Butte and admit that we've got houses of prostitution."

It was a bold move for the *Tribune* to run with the Beverly Snodgrass story. None of the other Montana papers were willing to publish it. But in October 1968, John Kuglin's seven-part series went to print with the *Tribune* printing an additional truckload to take to Butte, where residents scooped them up, hungry to read the national gossip that their town was stirring up. It was better than watching a soap opera. But the articles weren't so well-received by some.

The *Montana Post* lashed out, saying the *Tribune* had taken upon itself to "washing Butte's dirty linen." The editorial board asserted, "We strongly feel the *Great Falls Tribune*, in publicizing the ramblings of a prostitute, is pandering to sensationalism or yellow journalism . . . we believe the moralists are on insecure ground when they depend upon the apparently unsubstantiated story of a prostitute who claims she 'got religion.'" Individuals publicly dismissed Snodgrass's claims as personal revenge. Some argued it had blown up to an issue of political strong-arming between regional Democrats and Republicans.

John Kuglin was a respected Montana reporter who worked at various papers, eventually becoming the Montana/Wyoming Associated Press bureau chief. An article in Helena's *Independent Record* announced his retirement in 2005, describing Kuglin's diligent work throughout his career to uncover corruption in the state. He was at the forefront of the freedom of information campaign for open government that led to Montana's right-to-know constitutional provision, which some say is the strongest in the nation. His bold move to reveal the Beverly Snodgrass story tapped into a narrative of corruption that no one else was willing to touch. But even his October 1968 series kept a careful distance from the alleged perpetrators. The closest he came to actually naming Beverly's bench-sitting paramour was in calling him "a district judge" she had fondly called "Dimple Knees," or "Fancy Legs." Perhaps it was for liability purposes, to avoid the danger of making possibly inaccurate claims that lacked direct, damning evidence.

The Snodgrass story was a series of he-said-she-said exchanges between respected community leaders—men with honorable jobs and decent families—and a matron of the underworld who happened to have a heavy drinking problem. Whose word would the public be more likely to believe—city officials whom residents had voted into office, or some whacked-out whore who was rumored to have dyed her poodles in pastel colors? If, in fact, Beverly's claims were true, unscrupulous pillars of society were in the prime position to publicly discredit her assertions, writing her off as an unstable, punch-drunk lunatic with a personal vendetta. They could pull the necessary strings to distance themselves from their own dirty dealings, covering their tracks and avoiding public embarrassment, or worse, jail time for charges of corruption.

Apparently, the "whacked-out whore," despite the forces working against her, was able to scrape together and hold on to enough dope to really rattle some folks. Perhaps one of the most startling bits of evidence for Kuglin, personally, emerged after his series of stories ran. One evening he went out for beers with some buddies, when one of Governor Tim Babcock's aides saw him and pulled him aside, saying the governor requested to meet with him. According to Kuglin's account of his meeting with the governor, Babcock warned the reporter of a rumor he had heard circulating around: "They're going to get you. They're going to come over from Butte and kill you."

Subsequently spooked, as Kuglin put it, "I got a shotgun, loaded it, and stashed it under my bed."

As for Beverly, she returned to Butte shortly after her visit with senators Metcalf and Mansfield. In November 1968, the *Montana Standard* reported she had secured a loan from a local bank and was awaiting appointment to a state job. She eventually moved on to Boise, Idaho, then finally Walla Walla, Washington, where she lived out her remaining years. She died in 1987 at the age of sixty-five.

RUBY GARRETT—THE LAST BEST MADAM

Ruby Garrett was the last madam in Montana, outlasting Helena's Big Dorothy Baker by a decade. She was also known by her real name, Lee Arrigoni. Garrett was finally forced to relinquish control of the famed Dumas Hotel in 1982 after the local authorities and courts had brought considerable pressure to bear in the wake of crime associated with the place.

The Dumas had been built in 1892, practically designed for a fancy house of prostitution. In "Devil's Perch," historian Ellen Baumler explains how architects designed the building so a series of parlors and dining rooms "opened onto either side of a central hallway," and pocket doors were arranged so the entire space, with the door tucked away, could function "as a formal ballroom." The Dumas was run in 1900 by madam Grace McGinnis, who employed only four women, as did Lou Harpell in the Windsor Hotel. Having such a small number of women working was a luxury of the premier houses, catering as they did to the wealthiest clients. Their selection may have been small, but only the best women worked there.

Ruby Garrett deserves a proper entry in the catalog of colorful madams along with the many other women who had a sharp tongue, a lively wit, and a racy life. Few madams have the distinction, however, of having served a hitch in prison for homicide. According to the *Montana Standard,* Garrett killed her husband in 1959, after enduring too much of his physical abuse. News accounts say she shot him five times while he sat in a card game. Acquitted of murder, she was convicted on the lesser charge of manslaughter. According to witnesses, when Garrett entered the Board of Trade bar in Butte to shoot her husband, she had been beaten by him so badly that the men at the table did not recognize her. Her story must have garnered sympathy from the judge, if not the jury, since she served only nine months in the state penitentiary at Deer Lodge.

Her legacy at the Dumas began in 1971 when Garrett purchased the formerly illustrious hotel, telling the newspapers in 1982 that she was allowed to operate as madam for the monthly price of $300 payable to the police. According to historian Ellen Crain, Garrett was known in Butte for her kindness to the women who worked at the Dumas, and for running a clean and orderly business. She ran the Dumas as an establishment respectable enough to avoid the ire of the local community until 1981, when a violent robbery on the premises brought her into the news once again. This time the charges were technical, it seemed: tax evasion—the same crime that undid Al Capone. The result was that she was compelled to liquidate her interests in the Dumas on the eve of her departure for a federal facility in California, where she did a six-month sentence on the tax charge. As part of the agreement, she agreed to sell the Dumas. The *Montana Standard* profiled her farewell party in 1982, at the Melrose Bar south of Butte, as well-wishers and friends feted her. Baumler eulogized the demise of Butte's red light district succinctly, observing that with the sentencing of Ruby Garrett, "[p]rostitution, as Butte had known it, came to an end."

Ruby Garrett endured a while longer, however, as did the Dumas. In the early 1990s, Rudy Giecek purchased the property and promised to preserve its vibrant history somehow. Garrett herself told the *Montana Standard* in an interview in 1991 that "I know the old madams would be happy up there in heaven if they knew it was preserved." While many moralists might not share her optimism about the final destination of the "old madams," many Butte residents and Montanans in general share her sentiment for wanting to save an important aspect of Montana's past. As for the moralists, Garrett defended her career, saying of prostitution, "If you don't think it's

Ruby Garrett, who ran the Dumas brothel at 45 East Mercury Street in Butte, was the last known working madam in Montana when her business closed in 1982.
PHOTOGRAPH COURTESY OF THE BUTTE-SILVER BOW PUBLIC ARCHIVES.

morally wrong, it's kind of fun." In her view, "these little chippies who will do it for a burger and a beer, I say they might as well sell it."

Giecek tried to make a museum of the Dumas, forming an uneasy partnership with the International Sex Worker Foundation for Art, Culture and Education (ISWFACE) in 1998. In *Preserving Western History,* Andrew Gulliford quoted historian Ellen Baumler, Montana's premier representative of the National Register of Historic Places, as saying the Dumas was "not only significant as the last standing parlor house in this area of Butte, but also because of its length of operation as a rare, intact commentary on social history."

Madam Ruby Garrett's last outpost made headlines once again in 2005, when Giecek, who was leading a *New York Times* reporter on assignment through the hotel, supposedly discovered that a price-less collection of vintage and "rare sex toys" had been stolen from the building. According to Giecek, two thieves broke in through the back door and disabled the building's alarm system, then swiped irre-placeable items—apparently breaking apart beds, helping themselves to antique lamps and artwork, and clearing out glass display cases full of brothel artifacts. There have been some individuals, however, who claim Giecek was a fraudulent antiques dealer who had placed junk trinkets on display, claiming them to be authentic artifacts. Madam Ruby Garrett had signed affidavits claiming that Giecek's claims were false, since she had cleared the Dumas of all of her belongings before vacating the premises.

Today, the red brick building stands all but forsaken on Mercury Street, a fading monument to an earlier era and a parade of impressive madams who ran its rooms. Garrett herself died in 2012 in a Butte nursing home at the age of ninety-four. Not long before she died, she admitted that she might have made "different decisions" if she could live life over again.

"I don't think I would have become a nun," she said, "but I would have done some things different."

4

Great Falls

The Ladies of Rosebud Alley

From the 1920s until the 1960s, Great Falls was, after Butte, the most happening place in the state. It boasted the second-largest population (after Butte), and was intimately tied to Butte by the Anaconda Company. For years, much of the ore dug from the Richest Hill on Earth was processed on Smelter Hill, across the Missouri River from Great Falls in Black Eagle. In later years, Smelter Hill housed wire mills and other Anaconda Company subsidiaries. Like Butte, Great Falls could be a wild town, with fancy hotels and nightclubs and a steady traffic of bootleggers, gamblers, and other underworld figures enjoying the nightlife alongside some of Montana's most prominent citizens.

But even before Great Falls came into fame as one of the cultural and population centers of the state, it had a colorful past in terms of its nightlife. Retired professor Jay Moynahan's book, *Red Light Revelations*, provides a thorough overview of what he calls "Great

Falls' Lusty Past," from its incipience in 1884 to 1918, when prostitution was finally declared illegal.

One of the earliest of the prominent Montana prostitutes, Jew Jess, made her fame in Butte, although her success in Montana consisted largely in staying a leap ahead of the law. She worked out of Butte in the early 1880s as a thief and pickpocket but moved around the state frequently, usually at the urging of local police. She was also famous as a brawler, attacking other women with whom she was in competition. Though there's scant evidence that she was a madam in the strict sense, she did occasionally rent premises at which unsavory behaviors commenced, including opium smoking and prostitution. In 1889, the Great Falls police chief ran her out of town for the last time. She had apparently tried to establish a career in Great Falls, but her reputation as "the most notorious thief and confidence woman that ever visited the west," at least according to the *Great Falls Leader,* preceded her, and she was sent packing. The squib in the *Leader* concluded with a warning to her that "should she conclude to visit Great Falls again, she will hardly be given time to breathe the zephers [*sic*] from Black Eagle Falls." Great Falls was well acquainted with Jew Jess, or Jessie Lee, as she was also known, since she had been previously banished by the same chief in 1887. According to one *Leader* article reporting on that 1887 incident, Jew Jess had been apprehended in the company of "Annie Evans," the two of them having established an operation on Great Falls' famous Third Avenue South, also known as "French Row." Jew Jess would go on to achieve prominence as one of Butte's notorious characters of the line.

Another entry in the *Leader* in 1891 reported a fire "in a shack back of Maggie Hines' palace of sin on Third Avenue South and occupied by a colored woman named Mrs. Hattie Jones." Despite the implications, this reference is also too brief to establish that Hines was a full-fledged madam.

Great Falls had been founded by the prominent entrepreneur Paris Gibson, who laid out the streets and designed many of its buildings. He also served as one of the city's early mayors and signed city ordinances limiting prostitution, the first in 1888, which included the following language: "Any person . . . who shall invite or solicit any

Only high-class girls worked out of the distinctive Park Hotel, in downtown Great Falls.
PHOTOGRAPH COURTESY OF THE LIBRARY OF CONGRESS, HABS MONT,7-GREFA,1--1.

passerby to enter any bawdy house, house of ill fame or house of assignation [*sic*] . . . on conviction shall be fined not less than one dollar nor more than one hundred dollars." Several months later, Gibson
signed an additional ordinance that sought to eliminate "houses of
ill-fame" entirely, though business went on as usual, with "licensing
fees" paid to the appropriate authorities.

For the most part, the references in local papers collected by
Moynahan document the sordid lives of ordinary prostitutes who
were invariably called before the court on charges of vagrancy or corrupt morals, but also, often as not, as victims of violence from belligerent clients. Many of them made the papers for vicious fights—often
involving knifes and occasionally a gun—with jealous lovers or other
"Cyprians," as the newspapers delicately referred to them. These cases
usually resulted in a modest fine and the humiliation of the case being announced in the papers. In spite of Gibson's ordinances, madams continued to offer their services, and women continued to work
the streets.

In one particularly woeful case from 1901, a madam listed in the papers only as "Mrs. H. Johnson" apparently enlisted the services of sixteen-year-old Pearl Whitbeck, a crime for which Whitbeck was sentenced to a Miles City reformatory as "an incorrigible," while Mrs. Johnson was merely publicly shamed.

Because the founding of Great Falls happened much later than the earlier mining camps, the community bypassed the years of the hurdy-gurdys and crude log cabin cribs. Nevertheless, prostitution quickly gained a foothold, and Great Falls soon had a well-known demimonde just south of the central business district as early as 1887, only three years after the erection of the first downtown businesses.

In the mid-twentieth century, the hierarchy of prostitution applied in Great Falls as anywhere else: the high-class ladies worked out of Great Falls' finest and most expensive hotels, the Rainbow Hotel and the Park Hotel, both on Central Avenue in the heart of downtown. These women enjoyed privilege and income above the women of lesser houses, usually lower-quality hotels on side streets or in adjacent neighborhoods. In turn, even these parlor girls were better off than the streetwalkers, who worked out of the one-room cribs that they rented by the week. According to testimonies of erstwhile Great Falls prostitutes, the quality of the experience from the perspective of both client and supplier varied directly with the cost. The high-end girls invested time to ensure happy clients, priming them with fine whiskey and honeyed words, but low-rate women couldn't care less if the men failed to remove their boots to do the deed.

The tenderloin district of Great Falls was relegated to the area around the intersection of Second and Third Streets with Third Avenue North, a few blocks off of Central. However, when the Milwaukee Railroad relocated its headquarters to Great Falls, it contracted to erect a roundhouse and passenger depot precisely in this spot. In testimony to the community's acceptance of the reality of prostitution, if not outright approval of it, in 1913 a coalition of prominent businessmen, including the newspaper publisher O. S. Warden and lawyers for the Milwaukee Road, joined together to relocate the displaced women. The Great Falls Townsite company donated a few acres of land along an alley behind Tenth Avenue South and Second

Street, while the Milwaukee Railroad agreed to pay for the construction of new quarters for the women and their businesses. This section of town became known to locals as "Rosebud Alley." According to John Stephenson Sr., who penned an account of the deal, "The plan worked! The good ladies of the town were satisfied, and everybody was happy." That is, at least until 1917, when prostitution was officially criminalized and the site was rezoned for the city-county detention hospital.

Even though prostitution was officially illegal, and women had to worry also about enforcement of the 1910 Mann Act prohibiting transport of women across state lines for "immoral purposes"—a federal attempt to squelch the presumed trade in "white slavery"—things were different on a local level. In fact, a 1912 bookings ledger for the Great Falls Police Department reveals that the force regularly collected $10 fees from the working girls and $20 fees from the madams. In essence, the fees amounted to a quasi-legal license allowing these women the freedom to conduct business, although a sharper view would be that it amounted to nothing short of a protection racket. Evidently, ten percent of the proceeds went directly to the chief of police, while the rest of the revenue ended up in the city's coffers, a practice said to have persisted into the 1960s.

Legal prostitution in Great Falls came to a close when the trade was formally outlawed by the state in 1917 after Attorney General S. C. Ford, claiming he would reform Montana, was voted into office. Naturally, however, the practice persisted, much in the same way that alcohol still flowed more or less freely after the passage of the Volstead Act. The best evidence of prostitution's persistence may be found in a lengthy article in the *Great Falls Tribune* in January 1920, which bore the headline, "28 Women Are Arrested in Ten Rooming Houses." The establishments cited in the raids were a veritable catalog of the downtown hotels: the Daly Hotel, the Baatz Block, the Imperial Rooming House, the St. Paul Hotel, and the Armington Rooms, to name a few. Perhaps most striking about the 1920 raid was the unusual added ignominy of compelling all the women to undergo medical examinations, a process that revealed "Sixty Percent Found Diseased," as proclaimed in a subsequent headline later that same month.

Other Madams of Central Montana

A hundred miles to the northeast, Havre boasted its share of prostitution as well. The city emerged from the dust of the prairie in the last decades of the nineteenth century, as railroad baron James J. Hill enticed homesteaders to ride his Northern Pacific Railway trains into north-central Montana where they could claim free, 640-acre parcels of land. In fact, the county of which Havre is the seat is named for Hill.

It didn't take long for the world's oldest profession to gain a foothold in the blossoming community. The Great Falls Daily Tribune ran a lengthy article in April 1899 that reported great moral outrage over "women of the 'demi-monde' district" and the need for "remonstrance." In plain terms, what the upright citizens of Hill County demanded was "[t]hat all women be prohibited from entering any saloon or premises connected therewith; That women be prohibited from appearing on the public streets in improper attire; [and] To enforce all laws pertaining to 'bawdy' and houses of ill-fame."

In June 1908, under the "Police News" for the Havre Herald, a story reported that a house of ill repute had been raided near the Union Hotel, the ostensible madam being listed only as "Landlady Mrs. Swain."

Fergus County also boasted a few notable madams. According to a 2013 article in the Great Falls Tribune, Lewistown especially had a well-established red light district, with all the accompanying issues that went with it. In 1916, one boarding house was raided, yielding the arrests of twenty-two women.

On May 19, 1912, a young woman, Agnes Smith, with a sketchy past disappeared from Lewistown. The Great Falls Tribune speculated that "she may have ended her troubles and checkered career in the waters of the Missouri River." After all, she had long been associated with prostitution—and worse—had been arrested a few years prior for her part in a white slavery ring.

As had happened in Great Falls, by 1913, the Lewistown community was debating whether or not to relegate prostitution and the houses of the madams to a specific quarter of the town, as noted in the title of Civic Betterment Bulletin 1913: "Shall Lewistown Have a Segregated District?"

A few miles from Lewistown, in Moore, Montana, in 1907, a Mrs. Nora Johnson, identified as "a black woman" was mentioned in the Fergus County Democrat as running a house of ill repute, though she was eventually exonerated of the charges. In 1912, a relatively prominent court case focused on Grace Darling, Mary Doe, and Jennie Doe running a house of ill fame. A headline for February 6, 1912, revealed the result: "Jury Finds Darling Woman is Not Guilty: Exciting Case from Moore Attracts Interest When Time comes for Trial."

A few years earlier in Stanford, also in Fergus County, in 1907, Pearl West ran a house, for which she was arrested and compelled to pay a heavy fine.

BETTY ROGERS—BETTY'S PLACE

The most memorable and best known of Great Falls' madams appeared on the scene relatively recently. Great Falls eclipsed Butte as the largest city in Montana in 1950, but it had been growing steadily since the 1920s. In the 1940s, its entertainment and nightclub scene was probably more vibrant than even Butte's and was known throughout the West. With that reputation came some colorful women who ran some notable establishments.

According to one source, prostitute and madam Betty Rogers was the "longest working working-girl in the Electric City," a vivacious and flamboyant woman who began her career working for one of Great Falls' madams in the 1940s, Marion Marshall. Marshall operated a hotel upstairs from what had originally been the Murphy-Maclay Hardware store on Central Avenue. Though she would be arrested several times in her career, one of the earliest instances resulted in a headline in the *Great Falls Tribune* in December 1951: "Five Arrested in Raid, Prostitution Charges Filed." Rogers soon moved from being an employee to becoming an employer.

By 1958, Betty Rogers had taken over control of the establishment, known informally as "Betty's Place." Rogers was known for her colorful language and fondness for her dog, Lady, whom she used to sic on nosy neighborhood kids who tried to intrude on the premises.

According to a recent newspaper account, the jail's telephone number still remains on a wall next to where the telephone hung on an upstairs floor of the Rolfe Block where Rogers operated. She kept the number handy for contacting the police in the wake of an arrest of one of her girls, or to report an unruly or violent customer.

In 1958, local police raided Betty's Place. One of the more surprising discoveries during that raid was that police found copies of their shift schedules, some of which hung openly on Rogers' office walls. The best defense is a good offense, as the cliché has it, and Betty Rogers was a madam who knew that in her business, a good relationship with the law depended in part on good intelligence.

Whether as a matter of course or because the police felt slighted at seeing her keeping tabs on them, they arrested her and began a long campaign of harassment. One of the initial steps in that process was abatement proceedings initiated against the hotel. Abatement, defined in legal dictionaries as "the removal of a problem which is against public or private policy, or endangers others, including nuisances, such as weeds that might catch fire on an otherwise empty lot," was a standard tactic of the authorities who wished to limit or completely stop a madam's enterprises. Often the terms of abatement prohibited trespass, and Betty was arrested a few months later for breaking and entering after trying to return to what she considered her own premises.

Though she was routinely arrested or involved in altercations with the local authorities, Rogers considered herself a friend of the police. According to local historians (including a local businesswomen's group, the Downtown Chicks, who gathered oral histories from former acquaintances of Ms. Rogers), she was famous for having helped the FBI apprehend criminals who had passed through her hotel. On one occasion, for example, she was entertaining a client who suddenly became a little too rough for her liking. She boldly bit his index finger completely off, prompting the injured scoundrel to run bleeding from the room. Shortly after the incident, the FBI knocked on her door, since they happened to be in pursuit of the fellow who, it turns out, was much more dangerous than Rogers could have imagined. The agent leading the charge, Gene Fopp, expressed some frustration at having just missed the culprit.

"Cheer up," Rogers said, tossing him the finger. "You might find him in a hospital."

Though the incident took place years before the advent of DNA technology, the FBI at least had access to a fingerprint, thanks to Ms. Rogers. It turned out that the now four-fingered felon had been stealing cars along Montana's Hi-Line and bringing them to Great Falls to have their vehicle identification numbers filed off. Apparently, while waiting on his henchmen, the thief availed himself of the opportunity to enjoy a few hours at Betty's Place. Unfortunately for him, another patron had recognized him and tipped off the feds. The timing was impeccable, as Betty had just discovered for herself what a threat the man was.

In the end, you might say that Betty fingered the criminal, since, as she suggested, the police found him at a local hospital, bleeding profusely from the place where his erstwhile digit had been.

In one of her last court appearances, Betty Rogers behaved rather belligerently before the judge, prompting him to insist that the state investigate her mental condition. Great Falls residents had long gossiped about her antics among themselves. She was known to run errands around town clad only in a fur coat, with her dog, Lady, in tow, using an airline flight bag for a purse. She was also a legendary drinker known around Great Falls for a sharp and incautious tongue. Some reports suggest that Betty was eventually sent to the state mental institution in Warm Springs. How and when she died remains unknown.

BEA LAMAR—RIDING THE GRAVY TRAIN

Like Betty Rogers, Bea LaMar was one of Great Falls' most legendary madams. For many years, she was also a respected and prominent community figure, loved by many and known for her largesse and conversation.

The story of Bea LaMar begins with the Ozark Club, one of Montana's most famous nightclubs, known particularly for its jazz and its top-notch house band. One of the more interesting historical features of the club (which operated from 1933 to 1962) was that it was owned and operated by African Americans in a state that was more than ninety percent white. But as historian Ken Robison has noted, the Ozark Club "evolved from a 'colored club' into an entertainment sensation in a most improbable place—Great Falls, Montana." The club was located on Third Street South, nestled in among cafés, seedy bars, and houses of prostitution. The lower Southside was long associated with wild nightlife, including illegal drinking, gambling, and prostitution. When it opened in 1933, the Ozark sported a nightclub front, while the back rooms featured gambling, but it wasn't long before LaMar expanded into adjacent buildings, including a hotel next door, which he rechristened the LaMar Hotel. It was at the hotel, a logical extension of the infamous Ozark Club, that a lusty man might find the women working for the madam Bea LaMar.

Bea Lamar was the second wife of Leo Lamar, a charismatic and popular Great Falls personality. Leo had the grit and moxie to take a chance by opening Ozark just as Prohibition was ending. Leo LaMar had been a prizefighter, known as "Kid Leo," but it was his experience as a dining car waiter for the Great Northern Railroad that encouraged him to parlay his people skills into opening a nightclub for the African American community in Great Falls. Outside of a few clubs in Butte during the heyday of copper mining, the Ozark was one of the few venues in Montana designed to cater mainly to an African American clientele. By the 1940s LaMar desegregated the venue, according to Robison, opening the doors to all of Great Falls' citizens with the mottos, "All are welcome" and "Everyone's welcome, and will be there." This policy was in stark contrast to other local nightclubs, bars, and restaurants, where African Americans were excluded.

The Ozark Club retains a unique history as one of Montana's premier jazz clubs. The club offered a respected stage for famous and talented jazz musicians from all over the country to showcase their chops, the music often lasting until sunrise.

Meanwhile, in the LaMar Hotel near the nightclub, Leo's wife Bea LaMar plied her trade. The LaMars opened the LaMar Hotel in 1948 at 303 3rd Avenue South. The main floor housed Ellsberg Furniture. In the upper-floor rooms that had once been known as the Thompson Hotel, Bea became a madam, operating a prostitution ring that was known around Great Falls as "the Gravy Train," a moniker presumably coined by Bea herself. One source notes that Bea's slogan was, "We have it, We sell it, We still got it."

Leo LaMar, a former prizefighter, ran the famous Ozark Club, known for bringing top jazz musicians and singers to Great Falls. The house band was top notch, too.
PHOTOGRAPH COURTESY OF THE LAMAR FAMILY.

In contrast to Betty Rogers, who was loved for her sharp if somewhat crass tongue, the local community knew Bea LaMar as a distinctive and classy woman. According to oral histories collected by a branch of the Great Falls Preservation Players, who offer skits reenacting moments from Great Falls' red light history, Bea employed on average only a half-dozen girls at a time, and she treated them like royalty. Every Friday she took her employees by taxi to the Frances Beauty Parlor on Central to primp for the weekend, getting manicures, pedicures, and expert coiffures. Her girls charged between $7 and $22 for the services they provided, a figure that seems pitiful until you consider that minimum wage in 1950 was around one dollar. By contemporary standards, it was a premium wage for a woman of the night.

The LaMar Gravy Train may have pulled out of the station on its inaugural run with great fanfare, but the route did not operate long. In 1957, a disgruntled husband of one of LaMar's prostitutes shot a client, Richard Brown, as he left the premises, paralyzing the man. The jealous husband drew unwanted attention to the LaMar operation, derailing the Gravy Train for a period, and prompting a public trial. The trial itself was a routine affair, except for a most notable moment when the judge asked the gun-wielding husband, Glenn Totterdell, if he had any regrets about having maimed the man he had shot outside the LaMar Hotel. "I'm sorry I didn't kill the son of a bitch," replied Totterdell.

The publicity didn't do Bea LaMar any favors, especially since the unfortunate shooting had taken place just a couple of years after a well-publicized raid in 1955. This had led to a drawn-out court battle with the authorities, since one of the standard procedures the city followed was to abate the property and confiscate items of value. Eventually the LaMars recovered their confiscated cash and artworks, but their reputations were tarnished, and their prominence in the community diminished. The shooting returned the LaMar couple to the headlines, spawning further negative judgment. In 1957, Bea renamed the LaMar Hotel, perhaps to turn around her bordello's tarnished reputation, calling it the Doyle.

But things took a turn to the worst, retiring the Gravy Train to the roundhouse permanently in 1961 when Bea's stepson, Leo Jr., was killed in a car wreck, along with four others. The newspaper headlines for days afterward presented the shocking story to the Great Falls public.

According to an oral history from Margaret Murphy, however, which was collected by the Downtown Chicks, the story was a little more sordid than the newspapers let on. The fateful automobile ride had resulted from a bitter lover's quarrel. It seems Leo Jr. and a group of friends were partying at Bea's house on Lower River Road when Leo Jr. noticed that he was missing a valuable diamond ring. He accused one of the girls, twenty-five-year-old Yvette DuPre, of stealing it, but she assured him that he had simply left it at his own house.

Bea LaMar (foreground) ran a prostitution ring known as "the Gravy Train" out of the LaMar Hotel in Great Falls. PHOTOGRAPH COURTESY OF THE LAMAR FAMILY.

According to Murphy, what the newspapers left out was that when Miss DuPre climbed into the car in the wee hours for the fateful ride in search of the ring, she did so without donning a stitch of clothing. Consequently, when the police recovered the bodies at the wreck, she was completely nude. Nevertheless, at Croxford Funeral Home, the undertaker solved the mystery of the ring, since he discovered that she had stolen it after all, concealing the piece of jewelry in a very intimate part of her anatomy.

After that, life did not appear to get any easier for Bea. Within the following year, in 1962, her husband Leo died of a heart attack, and a short three weeks after that, the Ozark burned to the ground as fifty guests and staff fled for their lives. But the fates were not done with Bea quite yet. A month later, the madam received notice from the IRS that she owed $100,000 in back taxes on the Ozark. Bea had had enough. She renamed her establishment yet again, calling it the Vista Apartments. In 1966, she left Great Falls for good, moving to Livingston, and eventually landing in Billings, where she lived a quiet life working as a home nurse and becoming an active member of the local Catholic Church. She died in late summer of 1989 at the age of eighty-six.

In addition to the more colorful madams like Bea LaMar and Betty Rogers, Great Falls had numerous other, less prominent madams. In 1913, according to an article in the *Daily Missoulian,* a pair of "self-confessed white slavers" named Julia Metcalf and Mamie Wade pleaded guilty in a Great Falls court and were fined $400 and sentenced to four months in a Helena jail. The crime for which they had been arrested was bringing "three women from St. Paul to enter houses of ill-repute." In 1922, Edna Anderson was identified in the *Great Falls Tribune* as the owner of a known house of ill-repute. There was also Minnie Fisher, who ran a house in Fort Benton in the 1890s and figured prominently in a court case. Other cases involving putative madams are difficult to determine precisely. The headlines in early May 1922 in Great Falls chronicled the travails of "Mrs. Katcher," who "ran a boarding house" that her estranged husband insisted was a brothel. Their tawdry divorce played out in the papers, with Mrs. Katcher accusing Mr. Katcher of harassment, while he maintained that she was running a house of prostitution. She demanded alimony (since he was a prominent landowner) and claimed he had locked her out of her own Great Falls house. She also claimed he was a wife beater and said he criticized her operation. "All he did was to sit around home and find fault with the boarders and roomers," she said.

In *Great Falls: A Pictorial History,* authors Bill and Elizabeth Lane Furdell observed that "Great Falls, unlike many other western towns, was not the spontaneous product of some sudden discovery of gold, [but rather] the calculated creation of businessmen." The history of the demimonde in Great Falls in some ways mirrors the consciously devised plan of the city, as seen, for example, in the early creation of a specific red light district in close proximity to the downtown, and the deliberate relocation of that district to another part of the city with the express help of railroad and other business executives. But it also may be seen reflected in the cosmopolitan creation of the Ozark Club and the nearby LaMar Hotel, which were unusually canny business developments that capitalized on the end of Prohibition, a vibrant African American community, and a growing national appreciation of jazz music. In short, while the world's oldest profession may have remained a predictably available phenomenon, at least a few of the madams of Great Falls appear as surprisingly modern and in step with a new economy.

5

Missoula

Mary Gleim, the Flower of Garden City

M issoula, Montana, may be the best-known city in the state today, thanks to a university with a world-class writing program
and a national champion football team. It regularly makes top ten
lists as one of the most desirable places to live, and while it currently
boasts the second-largest population among Montana's cities, it is
poised to eclipse number-one Billings before long.

But it was not always so. For most of Montana's pioneer history,
and right up until the 1970s, Missoula (despite its brothels, gambling halls, and twenty-five saloons lining Ryman Street) played
handmaiden to Butte, which was the dominant force in Montana's
economy and its social and political history. Known as the "Richest
Hill on Earth," Butte was among the most boisterous and busy mining towns in America. All those mines needed massive amounts of
timber for lining shafts and reinforcing tunnels, and the early miners
quickly exhausted the available timber supply around Butte.

Missoula began as one of the most important mercantile locations on the Mullan Road that linked Fort Benton (the uppermost landing for steamboats on the Missouri) and Walla Walla, Washington (near the Columbia River). Conveniently located in a broad, flat plain where five valleys and three major rivers came together, Missoula provided a natural trading post location for early trappers and traders.

Long before the white man entered those valleys, Missoula was a camping ground for various Indian tribes, including the Salish and Flathead. The earlier fur trade routes stretched from what is now British Columbia to Colorado. Other routes flowed from tribes who lived east of the Continental Divide (Blackfeet and Crow) to carry on trade with tribes living west of the divide and near the coast.

After mining took off, Missoula also provided a natural location for lumber mills, as the valleys of western Montana, especially the Bitterroot and Flathead Valleys, were heavily forested. During Butte's most ambitious and lucrative mining years, Missoula furnished the bulk of the necessary timber.

Missoula also became a railroad town, a natural station on the cross-country route of the Northern Pacific Railway, as well as a station on the Chicago, Milwaukee, St. Paul and Pacific Railroad (aka the Milwaukee Road). The core of Missoula's prosperous downtown grew up along the railroad tracks, which still mark the northeastern edge of town and divide the main city from its quaint north-side neighborhoods.

Back in the day, those neighborhoods along the railroad tracks, especially in the vicinity of Alder and Spruce Streets, were home to Missoula's red light district. Even today, those downtown streets are lined with bars and restaurants, although the seedier taverns with besotted clientele have now given way to the college crowds who enjoy the lingering character of bars like The Silver Dollar and Al's and Vic's.

In the 1880s and 1890s, railroad tracks ran along the Clark Fork River, paralleled by Front Street, which was then the heart of the red light district. It was on Front Street that one of Missoula's most notorious madams, Mary Gleim, conducted business. She erected a Missoula landmark that still bears her name: the Gleim Building.

In the 1890s, Gleim hired architects and bricklayers to build a pair of brick buildings with elegant front-facing arches on West Front

Built in 1893, the Gleim Building still stands today at 265 West Front Street in downtown Missoula. PHOTOGRAPH COURTESY OF HENRY MULLIGAN.

Street. These brick edifices were to replace the wooden structures she had occupied earlier. An innocuous upgrade to the casual eye, her choice of brick reinforced her solid stand in the community of which she was a part. In spite of her questionable line of business, she had achieved the sort of success that justified a more permanent façade. At the same time, Missoula itself had come into its own and was shifting from the ramshackle and hastily thrown up false wood fronts that typified the western boomtown. Mary, like the town she occupied, intended to stay. Missoula, like many towns that had suffered debilitating fires, sought to preserve its downtown with fire codes that limited wood construction anyway.

Mary Gleim in fact made property development a substantial part of her business, and sources indicate that when she died in 1914, she owned land and property valued at more than $100,000, roughly $2.4 million in today's money.

In the pre-dawn hours of February 12, 1894, a man crept to the residence of Bobby Burns and stashed a few sticks of dynamite in a crawl space under his house. As the prominent West Front Street pimp lay sleeping in his bed, an explosion ripped through his home, jolting him and other residents of Missoula's red light district out of their slumber. Although the structure was reduced nearly to toothpicks, Burns remarkably stumbled away from the scene, thankful to be alive and fairly certain he knew the culprit behind this bungled attempt on his life.

Shortly thereafter, Burns posted a $500 reward for anyone who could provide him and local authorities with information about the perpetrators. Enough evidence came together to lead to the arrest of two men: Patrick Mason, a longtime resident of Missoula's red light district, and William Reed, a private who was stationed at Fort Missoula. That wasn't the end of it, however.

At the time, Mary Gleim, the reigning Front Street proprietress and entrepreneur of Missoula's underworld, was out of town managing other business affairs, and, according to her testimony, visiting the midwinter fair in San Francisco. Yet all fingers pointed to her as the brains behind the scheme to snuff out the man whom local papers identified as her "main rival."

*Gleim also owned the two-story Flatiron Building on Front Street, seen here in 1910
with women of questionable repute in the doorways.* PHOTOGRAPH "FRONT STREET OF MISSOULA"
1910 COURTESY OF THE HMFM NED L. MARSHALL COLLECTION (1992.008). USED BY PERMISSION. ALL RIGHTS
RESERVED.

She could hardly consider Burns an actual rival, however. He was
more like a small pimple on her ample back—the stocky, five-foot
six-inch, 170-pound Gleim was a dominating force in the district,
owning nearly all of the buildings running along West Front Street.
But she apparently did have it out for the man, once reportedly wrap-
ping a buggy whip around his neck before proceeding to drag poor
Burns through the street.

Following the explosion, unable to find anyone to provide her bail,
Mother Gleim was forced to hole up in a jail cell awaiting trial for her
alleged plot to murder Bobby Burns. To help pass the time in lock-up,
she managed to schlepp in a considerable liquor stash, which kept her
comfortably numb for the duration of her stay.

Her disdain for Bobby Burns was no secret. According to witness
testimony, Mary had on several occasions publicly conspired with
Patrick Mason to oust her longtime nemesis. One such scheme—
namely, a plot to poison Burns' sugar—could very easily have been
idle banter, cathartic chit-chat, so to speak. But in in the eyes of the
law, no real distinction lies between hypothetical conniving and
serious intent. That, in addition to Patrick Mason's loose lips, provided enough damning evidence to put Mother Gleim behind bars.

Previously a suspect himself, the key witness, William Reed, now accounted for every detail of the plot as told to him by Mason while they shared the holding pen awaiting trial. Both Mason and Gleim received fourteen-year sentences for attempted manslaughter, while Reed, because he had cooperated with authorities, was released on his own recognizance after posting bail of $1,000.

Notorious for her public outbursts and contempt for the law, Gleim surprised those seated in the courtroom that day. They fully expected the "Queen of the Badlands" to erupt upon hearing the jury's verdict on the case. Instead, as reported by the *Anaconda Standard*, "she took the sentence coolly and bridled her hitherto ungovernable tongue." The article concluded that her sentencing to the state penitentiary in Deer Lodge finally rid Missoula of "one of its most dangerous characters."

In a 2012 presentation for the Montana Historical Society, state archivist Jodie Foley proposed that the madam possibly remained uncharacteristically stoic because she had yet another hand left to play. Gleim's star-studded team of defense lawyers immediately filed for an appeal to the higher court, claiming that one of the jurors was not a United States citizen and that two of the prosecuting witnesses had been convicted felons. The Montana Supreme Court overturned the case and granted a retrial.

The game continued for yet another few hands, the luck of the draw going Gleim's way again and again. The madam indeed had the consummate final hand to play, whether intended or not. After two of the prosecuting team's star witnesses conveniently committed suicide, most of the other witnesses had skipped town, apparently fearful for their lives. But the crowning moment for Mother Gleim was learning that Bobby Burns, the only remaining material witness who could have had her locked away behind bars for fourteen years, would be unable to testify after all—he miraculously died of a heart attack.

Consequently, the case was dropped, and after serving just thirteen months of a fourteen-year sentence, the Queen of the Badlands was once again free to continue her reign over Missoula's red light district.

The wily and formidable madam starring in this scandalous tableau was born Minnie Winifred Gleeson in Tipperary, Ireland, in 1846.

She claimed her father had been a squire who saw to it that she had a solid, well-rounded education, but everything about her abusive nature as an adult indicates that her life was probably very difficult while growing up. She was a small child in Ireland in the midst of the devastating potato famine, for example, and it is reasonable to infer that her irascible character as an adult stemmed from the deprivation and stress of her early life. As she became a young woman, she cleverly situated herself to improve her financial standing, doing what she could to shield herself and get ahead.

At twenty-four, she had a sweetheart—John Edgar Gleim, a St. Louis native from a well-to-do family, who was no stranger to the jailhouse due to his thirst for liquor and his gambling appetite. They happened to be in Sussex, England, when they wed, and theirs proved an ideal partnership: Mary had promised to tend to the family finances so John could drink and gamble to his heart's content. What's more, she proved that she had an instinctive talent for making more money out of the funds her husband entrusted to her. After building up their fortune in St. Louis—presumably in the sex trade—the couple moved to Missoula in 1888. Mary opened a female boarding house on Front Street and posted a euphemistic ad in the local paper to draw in prospective patrons:

> Mrs. M. Gleim begs to inform the public that she has returned from Chicago with two carloads of the newest and latest styles in furniture. Having more than she requires for her new lodging house, she will sell bedroom sets at cost price. . . . No reasonable offer will be refused.

Apparently business was such a success in that town of bachelors that within a year, Mary scooped up eight more properties on West Front Street and officially established herself as the matron of Missoula's red light district. But as her empire expanded and the list of her properties lengthened, so did the list of her enemies.

Mary Gleim appeared in the local papers so often for her run-ins with the law and with fellow citizens that she may as well have had her own weekly column. Time and time again, she was called into court for owing employees and contractors back pay (even though she was quick to evict any tenants who did not keep current with what was owed her). She was, in short, a brutal force to be reckoned with, according to author Matthew P. Mayo in his book *Hornswogglers, Fourflushers & Snake-Oil Salesmen: True Tales of the Old West's Sleaziest Swindlers.* He claims the madam was not kind to the women who worked for her. "She routinely beat them, cheated them out of their pay, and forced them to live in unacceptable conditions," he says. "Perhaps she was afraid she wouldn't have enough money to pay her lawyers for her constantly renewed dates." But despite these stories about how she unfairly treated the hired help, Mary Gleim was said to have paid for the education of aspiring businessmen and lawyers (possibly to secure future favors), as well as for the young women of her houses who wanted to improve their chances at self-efficacy, perhaps harboring a fondness for the ambition she herself expressed at an early age.

Gleim considered herself, above all, a businesswoman, and she did very well for herself financially, although a considerable portion of her business dealings were nefarious. One article from the *Livingston Enterprise* in June 1890 reported that she was arrested in New York for smuggling goods. She reportedly dealt not only in the skin trade, but also in the smuggling of opium, lace, and diamonds, and was said to have been smuggling in Chinese laborers via an underground railroad connection running out of Thompson Falls. Some of her more legitimate ventures, on the other hand, involved such mundane enterprises as buying and selling real estate and making bricks.

In any case, one gets a sense that, whatever her professional dealings, Mary had a short fuse, with little patience for stupidity, and she was downright terrifying when angry. According to Montana Historical Society archivist Jodie Foley, Gleim was a "relentless hater," which would be apparent to anyone scrolling through the newspaper archives documenting the madam's interactions with the law and her rivals.

In January 1892, for example, she laid into two men of the cloth as she entered a church with a strong smell of liquor on her breath to pay her respects to the "McCormick child," a child who had recently died. As she was well versed in all of the Romance languages, Mary inquired, in Latin, to Father Jay Neill and Brother Pascal Magazinni as to why they had not set out a candle for parishioners to light for the girl's soul. Neither priest responded as their knowledge of Latin was perfunctory and limited to saying the mass. Incensed at their ineptitude, Mother Gleim whipped herself into a tirade and proceeded to rip the frocks off their backs. After smashing some of the furniture, she exited the holy place.

But she was not quite done with her revilement. Upon climbing into the carriage awaiting her outside, she unleashed on the poor hack driver, beating him repeatedly as well. According to Foley, Mother Gleim later testified in court that she informed the priests that "they aught to learn the language where Romulus and Remus were suckled by the wolf on the banks of the Yellow Tiber." She claimed they were unfit to wear such holy raiment. "I don't believe there are any genuine priests in this country," she told the court. According to her story conveyed at the stand, she was heading toward the door to leave, when she tripped and grabbed Father Neill's robe to soften her fall. The court didn't buy it, so Gleim was hit with three assault charges.

The spring before Gleim was accused of masterminding the attempt on Bobby Burns' life, a May 1893 *Helena Independent* article reported that one of Gleim's customers, Charles McLeod, had overdosed on morphine. A doctor by the name of Hansen had attempted to resuscitate the man on the floor, but Mary stormed over and pointed a pistol at the doctor, escorting him off the premises. When the doctor was later able to return to assess the man's state of health, the victim was too far gone, and he died. Later, Dr. Hansen declared that the madam was essentially responsible for the man's death, and that had she not driven the doctor away from McLeod, the victim would likely have survived. Mother Gleim wound up awaiting trial in the county jail.

After her release from prison, 1895 continued to be a year rife with confrontation for Gleim. Apparently, the madam was itching to release some of her pent-up aggression. Two weeks after walking out of jail a free woman, she got into a squabble with one of her house ladies, French Emma. According to the article that appeared in the *Daily Missoulian,* the madam nearly killed the young woman, who, coming out of the fight, "resembled a high piece of decorative art, her eyes black and swollen with a deep brown colored oil painting covering the side of her face. One of her hands was badly lacerated, said to have been done by Mrs. Gleim's teeth." According to Mary's testimony, Emma had planned to kill her, as evidenced by the knife that fell out of the young woman's dress. Had she not trounced the girl in self-defense, argued Gleim, she would be dead as a result of a revenge scheme orchestrated by none other than the deceased Bobby Burns.

Soon after, she assaulted her husband's right-hand man, Billy Preneveau, who was "a total wreck" after she punched him in the cheek, knocked him down, and hammered him to a pulp with a table leg. Perhaps such violence was simply Mary's way of dealing with her frustrations over her husband's failing health. Shortly after her release from Deer Lodge, John died from complications of chronic gastritis. He left a sizable homestead back in St. Louis, which the Gleim family had acquired when John's grandfather married a Wisconsin Indian. It was tribal property, and because John and Mary had no children, the plot of land by law reverted back to other family members. Despite having lost this sizable parcel of property, Mary Gleim continued to expand her holdings and build her business.

In 1905, when Mary was nearly sixty, she was faced with yet another possible prison term. She was indicted this time for assault with intent to kill after she and two men reportedly broke into the home of a man by the name of C. A. Clayton and "cruelly and maliciously" bashed him on the shoulders, face, and head. The madam fell back on her old "self-defense" plea and was, yet again, miraculously found not guilty for her aggression. (She was known on more than one occasion to publicly celebrate the verdicts she more or less bought.)

Mother Gleim continued to terrify people with her temper when she was well into her late sixties. An April 1913 article in the *Daily Missoulian* reported an incident in which she let loose on a gentleman by the name of Pat Henegan, who helped himself into her home with the intent to swipe a few of the madam's personal belongings. Upon discovering her intruder, Mary chased him into a corner, threatening him with a stove poker if he dared move. A passerby heard the fracas from outside and fetched the police. When the man and

At the Missoula City Cemetery, Mary Gleim's headstone is gilded with lichen.
PHOTOGRAPH COURTESY OF HENRY MULLIGAN.

accompanying officer raced back to the scene, they were met by Henegan, who had somehow managed to escape. He begged them for protection from the madam, because he feared for his life. Henegan was subsequently locked up, safely, in the county jail.

In February 1914, Mother Gleim fell ill with influenza and died. Her estate was valued at more than $100,000, all of which she left to her Irish niece and nephew whom she had brought to the United States in order to raise them when they were young. The two heirs paid $700 for an enormous headstone in the Missoula City Cemetery, which faces west toward the railroad tracks, in contrast to all the other grave markers there facing north and south. Legend has it that Mary wanted the headstone of her final resting place to face those tracks, so she could "wave to her boys"—the railroad workers who had always been her best customers.

A more likely but less romantic explanation, however, is that the headstone was simply too large to place on the grave as the others were, so it was turned sideways to accommodate the space.

6

The Madams of Miles City and Billings
Untamed Women on an Untamed River

The longest free-flowing river in the lower forty-eight states, the Yellowstone begins its nearly 700-mile descent from Two Ocean Plateau in Wyoming and tumbles northward, needling between the Absaroka and Gallatin mountain ranges, and on past Livingston, where it slides past the city of Billings. It then progresses northeastward, rendezvousing with the Tongue River at Miles City, which lies far to the east of the historically older towns of Missoula, Helena, and Butte. The river eventually spills into the upper Missouri in North Dakota. Much hasn't changed with this wild and scenic river, and it likely looks very much the same to us today as it did to the women who plied their trade in the wild towns that sprung from its banks back in the days of the Montana Territory.

After Lieutenant Colonel Custer's 700-man battalion fell in 1876 to the Lakota, Northern Cheyenne, and Northern Arapaho Indians at the Battle of Little Bighorn, Colonel Nelson A. Miles founded the Tongue River Cantonment at the confluence of the Yellowstone and

Tongue Rivers, a military post established to prevent the "untamable" Sioux and Cheyenne from escaping across the border up to Canada. Although Miles managed to subdue the tribes of the area, he realized a much bigger problem within the confines of his own camp. His soldiers had taken a fervent liking to the "liquid stock."

In his book *Saloons of the Old West*, author Richard Erdoes states, "It has been jokingly said that, with the exception of the Battle of the Little Bighorn, all western history was made inside the saloons, and there is a grain of truth in this." Free-flowing whiskey was causing Colonel Miles more grief than were the Indians, so he cut off his men's supply by banishing the garrison merchants to a location two miles east, where they founded the original Miles City. The colonel soon moved his men to higher ground at the newly constructed Fort Keogh, two miles west of the confluence. As a result, the whole town of Miles City relocated back to the original settlement site at the confluence, where the town of 8,400 is situated today.

In the 1880s, Miles City was a wild livestock town where Texas cattlemen drove their herds to fatten up on the wide open grasslands before loading them onto trains headed to the Chicago slaughterhouses. By 1881, the town was flush with boarding houses, brothels, and dance halls, not to mention forty-two saloons quenching the thirst and soaking the minds of its 1,000 residents. A visiting judge, taken aback by the number of fights he witnessed, claimed it was an utterly "demoralized and lawless" place where the streets were "unsafe at night."

One of the greatest of the cowboy memoirs is *We Pointed Them North*, by Teddy "Blue" Abbott, who spent a fair amount of time in Miles City. In his book, Abbott talks openly of his acquaintance with the women of the red light and is frank in his relaxed attitude about the prevalence of the world's oldest profession in eastern Montana. In Abbott's view, women in the trade in Montana had a better life and reputation than their counterparts back East.

"I used to talk to those girls, and they would tell me a lot of stuff, about how they got started, and how in Chicago and those eastern cities they wasn't allowed on the streets, how their clothes would be taken away from them, only what they needed in the house, so it

Teddy "Blue" Abbott appears ready to spin a yarn as he hand rolls a cigarette.
PHOTOGRAPH COURTESY OF THE BILLINGS PUBLIC LIBRARY, BPL2013.01.001.

was like being in prison," said Abbott. "They could do as they please out here."

A great part of Abbott's firsthand experience came from a period of eight or nine days he spent recuperating from being thrown off a horse in 1884. His boss, the famous cattleman Zeke Newman, sent him to Miles City to mend. "Oh boy, but life was good," wrote Abbott. "There were girls there that I had seen at a lot of different places along the trail. They followed the trail herds. The madams would bring them out from Omaha and Chicago and St. Paul; you would see them in Ogallala, and then again in Cheyenne or the Black Hills."

Miles City had developed quite a reputation for its nefarious nightlife, with rail workers, laborers, riverboat men, and cow punchers packing the throng of night venues. The red light district was located at the end of Pleasant Street, near the river, with houses of ill fame operating up until the 1960s, when they finally shut down for good. According to Amorette Allison, Miles City historic preservation officer, madams were charged monthly fines or process fees, payable to city officials, up until the 1960s in order to keep their doors open to the public. The community came to rely on those funds coming in. "Madam money kept the city running through the depression," she said.

From the start, wealthy Miles City madams were known to stake legitimate business ventures as well as subsidize major construction projects for the community, such as the Bullard Block on Main and Sixth, which eventually housed Montana's first telephone exchange, providing a direct connection to Fort Keogh's telegraph line.

Meanwhile, 150 miles upstream, Billings (today, Montana's largest city) also had a thriving red light district and had developed quite a reputation of its own. Dubbed the "Magic City" for its rapidly growing population built around the railroads, Billings (like Great Falls) was platted by the Northern Pacific Railway on the Yellowstone River at the foot of an impressive bluff rising to the north of town known as the Rimrocks.

The Northern Pacific Railway completed its transcontinental line through Montana in 1883. That same year, the Billings Land and Irrigation Company opened the "Big Ditch," a thirty-eight-mile canal bringing water from the Yellowstone River to the parched benches of the city and adjacent lands. A system of ditches and canals soon provided water throughout the area for both irrigation and domestic use. Land agents sold property to hopeful settlers, and the town quickly grew.

The town was named for Frederick Billings, the outgoing president of the railroad who invested heavily in the project and was the chief stockholder. Thanks to the federal government's liberal land grants, the railroad barons essentially manufactured a ready-made city on a stretch of some of the most prime real estate along the Yellowstone.

Within a few years of Billings' founding, the first mention of its red light district and "houses of ill fame" appears in the historical record. The original brothels and cribs lined both sides of the railroad tracks, but business soon concentrated along four blocks of Minnesota Avenue between South 27th and South 23rd Streets. This became known as the "restricted district."

Mattie "Kit" Rumley was the first madam to establish a presence in Billings in 1883, with a rush of ladies working the skin trade soon to follow. The renowned Ollie Warren arrived a decade later, establishing a house called the Lucky Diamond at 2512 Minnestoa Avenue, right in the heart of the restricted district.

The first attempts to curtail the skin trade in Billings came in 1898, when various ordinances suppressed prostitution and outlawed vagrants, particularly women who behaved in an "immodest, drunken, profane or obscene manner," which pretty much described any Billings courtesan.

Attempts to close down the sex trade paralleled the push for Prohibition and new moral standards. The influx of soldiers during World Wars I and II also raised concerns about sexually transmitted diseases. In 1918, a military officer warned officials that twelve hours in Billings rendered a potential recruit unfit for military service. "I am talking about your line of cribs where naked women lean over window sills and entice young boys in for fifty cents or a dollar," he said. "Close that south-side line in twenty-four hours, or the military will move in and do it for you."

At the tail end of World War II, the Federal Security Agency requested that cities across the country close their red light districts to help prevent the spread of venereal diseases among soldiers passing through or stationed in their towns. Men on active duty were prohibited from visiting the cathouses; however, that didn't completely stop the spread of disease. One 1943 article in the *Billings Gazette* reported that cases of VD dropped fifty to seventy-five percent within army and navy communities where brothels had been closed. In 1943, Mayor Harry E. Biddinger announced the shuttering of the Magic City's red light district and issued a statement that "rooming houses and hotels would be contacted and warned about the impending closure." He insisted that eliminating the first line of vice would rein in the problem of infection, and pledged agency efforts would ensure that the "ladies of the evening [would] find it unprofitable to remain after the district [was] closed. This was no small feat, as soldiers knew within minutes of de-boarding the train just where the red light resided.

Condemning the soiled doves of Billings in such a manner was not really the full solution to the problem. According to the local sanitary inspector at the time, only one percent of infections were reported to have originated in the district. The other ninety-nine percent reportedly came from "victory" girls—young women (even teenaged girls) who professed their patriotism by traveling to various encampments or ports during wartime mobilization and charitably offering their bodies to the men in uniform.

Prostitution in Billings—as well as throughout Montana—persisted, despite attempts to end the trade. Boxes upon boxes of district attorney files, available at the Montana Historical Society, reveal records of operating brothels on the outskirts of town, in outlying areas, and everywhere in between. Even Billings' local channel KULR-8 news station reported back in 2013 that a red light district was evident as recently as the 1990s, where on any given night, fifteen to twenty women paraded along Montana Avenue, sandwiched between Billings' original district on First Avenue and its modern counterpart on Minnesota Avenue—right where Ollie Warren's Lucky Diamond operated. For the town and river alike, the more things change, the more they stay the same.

Could this be Fannie French's brothel? The scene was shot in Miles City circa 1905, and the women are wearing "Mother Hubbard"–style gowns typical of prostitutes of the day.

FANNIE FRENCH—
A WOMAN TO BE RECKONED WITH

When she was just sixteen years old, Fannie Hendrix—known today as Fannie French—got a job as an army scrubwoman at Fort Keogh. She was a biracial beauty, with her mother hailing from England and her father from New York. Like many women who washed uniforms for soldiers by day, she worked evenings tending to the desires of those men for a price, and she eventually collected a big enough coffer to quit her job at the compound and purchase a house in Miles City, on the south side of Main between Sixth and Seventh, where she discreetly managed a bordello. Her parlor came to be known as "Fanny French's Negro House," catering to darker-skinned clientele, namely soldiers and railroad men.

Fannie was a sharp woman—she could read and write and had strong business acumen. As her enterprise grew, so did her house, and by 1882, she opened a new parlor on Bridge Street, which boasted a ballroom with a piano, eleven bedrooms, and a "yellow-skinned" woman to work each one. She was even able to purchase her own livery and, as an expert horsewoman, enjoyed riding out on the range in her free time.

In late November 1885, Fannie was indicted for "lewd and boisterous behavior while running a house of ill fame." But she didn't take her $300 fine and three-month jail sentence sitting down. Appealing her case all the way to the Montana Supreme Court, Fannie contended that a *reputation* for running a whorehouse is not grounds for conviction: one has to have *evidence* that a person is running a whorehouse. She did not win her case; however, the court removed the jail sentence, and the madam had officially established herself as a force to be reckoned with in Miles City.

About eight years later, Fannie French became the first person formally tried for a criminal case in Custer County. In the early morning hours of January 11, 1892, a client by the name of Jeremiah Majors got into an altercation with one of Fannie's ladies. The young woman was his favorite of the house, but Fannie had already promised her to another client. Majors had a fit and proceeded to grab the woman by the hand, to pull her forcibly upstairs while elbowing Fannie to get by. Quick to react, Fannie grabbed a leather strap that lay on a nearby chair. She whipped Majors to unconsciousness. When in court, she claimed to be defending herself and her property "against the threat of force and mayhem." Instead of sentencing her for assault, she got off on a misdemeanor. Apparently, she had close ties with several of the jurors. After an original vote of ten to acquit and two to convict, and after much deliberation, jurors agreed on a compromise. Fannie went home without having to serve time, but was required to pay a $50 fine.

Fannie had three children—Birdie, Nora, and Charles—but they were not reported to have been hanging around their mother's place of business. In 1894, however, the *Yellowstone Journal* did note that her daughter Birdie Astle was the first resident of the city to be sent to reform school.

Fannie ran her brothel in Miles City for twenty years before moving to Billings to live out the remainder of her life. According to the 1900 Billings census, she was running a house right in the heart of the red light district. She died of dropsy (likely congestive heart failure) in June 1901. Her daughter Nora came to Billings to tend to her mother's remains.

MAGGIE BURNS—
A RED-HEADED FIGHTING SON OF A GUN

The winter of 1884 in Miles City loomed large in Teddy "Blue" Abbott's memory, as he and two companions spent considerable time lounging at Mag Burns' parlor house. Burns was one of Miles City's most successful madams, arriving sometime around 1880, after her lover, William Bullard—who happened to be serving as county sheriff at the time—convinced her to leave her career as a successful prostitute in Deadwood, South Dakota, and relocate to this burgeoning town. She opened the first white bordello, called the "44," which was located on Seventh Street between Main and Bridge. The beautiful women she recruited from Deadwood catered mostly to a crowd of cattle barons and ranchers.

While Teddy "Blue" and the madam were ordinarily on good terms, one incident became famous in the annals of Montana's nightlife, immortalized even in one of Charlie Russell's "Rawhide Rawlins" yarns. As Abbott explains, he and two companions, John Bowen and Johnny Stringfellow, had gotten drunk and were attempting to play music in Mag's parlor.

"John Bowen was playing the piano and he couldn't play the piano, and Johnny Stringfellow was there sawing on a fiddle and he couldn't play fiddle, and I was singing, and between the three of us we was raising the roof." The cacophony was too much for the proprietor of the business, whom Abbott describes as "the redheaded, fighting son of a gun," and she became incensed. "If you leather-legged sons of bitches want to give a concert, why don't you hire a hall? You're ruinin' my piano!" she cried.

Her disdain for their merrymaking in turn incensed Abbott, who went outside and mounted his horse, Billy, and rode him into Mag's parlor. The madam locked Teddy and his horse in the house and called the police, but Abbott spurred his horse through an open window and rode for the ferry, upon which he dashed with his horse and escaped

Teddy "Blue" Abbott, left, cut quite the dapper figure posing here with artist Charlie Russell. PHOTOGRAPH COURTESY OF THE MONTANA HISTORICAL SOCIETY RESEARCH CENTER, 940-046.

to freedom. By the next day, the affair had blown over, and he was again welcome at Mag's house.

Interestingly, Abbott recalls several frank conversations with Mag's girls about the profession. He remarked to a woman identified only as "Myrtle," that "before I was married, I used to hop around among you folks a good deal, and I don't see how you stand it. It looks like a hell of a life to me." But Myrtle surprised him with her response: "There's a kind of fascination about it. Most of the girls that are in it wouldn't leave it if they could."

Abbott seems surprisingly feminist for the age in which he flourished as well. "I've heard a lot about the double standard, and seen a lot of it too," he wrote, "and it don't make any sense for the man to get off so easy. If I'd have been a woman and done what I done, I'd have ended up in a sporting house."

The double standards abounded, really. Abbott quotes Mag Burns herself, who said that "the cowpunchers treated them sporting women better than some men treat their wives."

Another Miles City madam Abbott discusses was Willie Johnson, a madam whom he defended from a disgruntled customer by holding him at bay with his pistol. Evidently the fellow Abbott threatened to shoot if he came any closer to Johnson was her sweetheart, and in a lover's quarrel, he had blackened her eye and inflicted a cut on her forehead that was bleeding profusely. As Abbott doctored her wound, he tried to console her.

"I don't care for the black eye, Teddy," she told him. "But he called me a whore." Abbott chalked that irony up to the hazards of the profession itself. His memoir is perhaps unusual in his staunch defense of the madams and their employees as business people like any others. He praised their integrity and marveled at their pugnacity in the face of adversity.

As for Maggie Burns, she made huge profits and bankrolled Bullard's venture into brewing beer, which also proved successful. She reportedly sold the "44" to one of her employees, Connie Hoffman, and eventually married Bullard, and the two headed off to settle on a farm in Corpus Christi, Texas.

ETTA FEELEY— A RUGGED STAR IN A RUGGED LAND

A little, one-story cobblestone house sits beside Bennett Creek—just outside the small, unincorporated community of Clark, Wyoming—which bubbles along in a two-mile trek northwest before it converges with the Clark's Fork of the Yellowstone River. The little house is situated on property near the Shoshone National Forest and Clark's Fork River Canyon. A woman of simple means once lived there in solitude in the mid-1940s, with only her two horses as companions. The property lies a little over 100 miles south of Billings, where the woman had spent some years in her younger days. Towering in the backdrop are the ragged peaks of the Beartooth Mountains on the edge of the Bighorn Basin. The Crow wintered in that area because little snow, clear skies, and big game made it an ideal haven during the colder months. The Beartooths' majestic beauty comprises 10,000-foot plateaus and more than twenty-five peaks rising above 12,000 feet. More than 300 natural lakes and waterfalls are tucked throughout the range, where grizzlies, black bears, moose, elk, mountain goats, bighorn sheep, mountain lions, lynx, wolverines, and wolves all make their home.

Alice Leach was a rugged woman living in rugged territory.

She never learned to drive a car. A stout woman, she usually wore slacks, a simple blouse, and a vaquero hat, and she found herself most comfortable while seated astride one of her equine friends. Even when she was well into her eighties, she was known for having made long trips on horseback up to Billings via Red Lodge, or south to Cody, Wyoming. In her younger days, she was known to haul four-horse loads of beer from Red Lodge to Cody. But her advanced years made her less inclined to want to travel much away from home, so for the simple necessities, she gave her lists to the mail lady, a resident of the neighboring town of Belfry, who brought her groceries and supplies on the next delivery day. On those rare occasions when Mrs. Leach did leave the house and head into town, the locals never saw her dolled up in a dress, but she had applied a thick layer of brightly colored lipstick—a wee indicator of the life she once led.

This mountain woman had not always been poor. She came from a well-heeled family, but also did very well for herself in her chosen career. As a former madam, Etta Feeley maintained prominent houses of prostitution in Sheridan and Cody, Wyoming, as well as in Billings.

She was born Alice M. Edwards in Iowa, sometime around 1870, to Henry Clay Edwards and May Doxey. May came from a close-knit family of wealthy farmers, and she married Henry at her parents' homestead in Washburn, Iowa. Henry, the son of a doctor, was a blue-coat veteran of the Civil War who tried his hand at farming to support his young bride and infant daughter, but his efforts to work the land met with only marginal success. By the time of the 1880 federal census, he had relocated his family to Fort Collins, Colorado—just about the time the Colorado Railroad arrived to bring a flood of

This tintype of Alice Edwards at age five or six offers no hint of the life she would lead.
PHOTOGRAPH COURTESY OF THE FAY KUHLMAN COLLECTION FROM THE ESTATE OF ALICE EDWARDS LEACH,
PARK COUNTY ARCHIVES, PO2-15-27.

newcomers and promise to that agricultural town. Henry listed his occupation as a "teamster," which meant that he drove horse-drawn wagons carrying and delivering goods. It was a job common for those considered to be "unskilled laborers," although that pejorative hardly captures the scope of their duties. Not only were teamsters responsible for making deliveries, but they were expected to care for their horse teams, balance the books, account for lost or stolen goods, and collect on overdue debts. Their employers often took advantage of them, demanding that they work extremely long hours with little to no reimbursement. Such an existence likely took a toll on his marriage, and May, with her affluent upbringing, lost patience with the financial struggles and attendant stresses. She was a woman of action who wanted more than a subsistence living for her child, so she took young Alice back home to Iowa to live with her parents.

Alice first made the news in 1886 when she was just fifteen or sixteen. While she was at her grandparents' home, a neighboring farmer, Simon Clacy, came around for a visit. According to an article in the local paper, Clacy suddenly grabbed her and tried to plant a kiss. Although the newspaper account suggested that in retaliation she "playfully" grabbed a gun from a nearby cupboard and shot the man, one has to wonder how "playful" Alice considered Clacy to be in his manhandling of her. The bullet pierced his liver, leaving him crumpled on the floor with "little hope for recovery." She was never tried for murder.

In October 1889, records indicate that she ran off to Boise, Idaho, to marry a baker, Walter C. McGinn. It is likely that Boise was merely a wedding location, as Walter was listed in the Portland, Oregon, *City Directory* at that time. Alice's name, as well as her known assumed names, never appeared in any Portland or Boise directories during these years. In 1891, however, Walter's name dropped from the Portland book and appeared in a Denver listing—a baker with an identical name, right down to the middle initial.

According to an article in the summer 2013 *Cody County Legends*, Alice got her start working in a theater in Denver in the early 1900s. At some point, she adopted the name Etta Feeley. A 1960 society pages insert in the *Billings Gazette* included an article by Fay Kuhlman highlighting Feeley's life, noting that the famed Billings "roadhouse" owner got her start in "show business," with a "sensational career" as a "model and actress" in other western cities before landing in Billings. (This article never once discusses the true essence of her profession.) There's a good chance that "show business" was a euphemism

No public records are known to tie Etta Feeley to Portland, Oregon, but the portrait on the left, taken around 1891, shows her posed in a studio at 283 First Street, in the heart of Portland. Around the same time, she also sat for the high fashion portrait on the right, taken at the Tritz studio in Waterloo, Iowa. PHOTOGRAPH COURTESY OF THE FAY KUHLMAN COLLECTION FROM THE ESTATE OF ALICE EDWARDS LEACH, PARK COUNTY ARCHIVES, PO2-15-48 AND PO2-15-10 A&B.

for dance hall, or burlesque theater. She may have used an assumed name and may have moved frequently from town to town, as did many women in her profession. An article in *Cody County Legends* explains that she often performed in a swing, raised high above the crowd, wearing pink tights and provocative costumes that showed off her slender waistline. Although the Denver city directories contain no listings for either Alice Edwards or Etta Feeley around that time, a Kate Feeley does appear in 1899 listed as a resident of some "furnished rooms"—a common euphemism for whorehouses of the day— located on Champa Street. It would not be an unreasonable stretch to think that Kate Feeley could be a pseudonym for the very same woman who eventually took the similar moniker—Etta Feeley.

Kuhlmann writes that Etta first arrived in Billings in 1892, and the whole town felt "charged" with the news of her arrival. Another source indicates she went to work in a high-class gentleman's house. This "house" might very well be the place Kuhlman mentions as the Bennett Theater, at which Etta was known to perform. No city directories from that time period list a venue specifically by that name, but according to the *Montana Gazetteer and Business Directory* of 1896, a man named W. J. Bennett is listed as the proprietor of the B&B Vaudeville and the Cameo Theater. The Cameo exhibited full-page ads that boasted its "first-class vaudeville troupe" along with a restaurant and the "finest brands of liquors and cigars." In directories of later years, Bennett was listed as a saloon man on the 2700 block of Minnesota, right in the heart of Billings' demimonde district. It would be reasonable to assume that Etta Feeley was under his employ in her early years as a Billings "star."

Once the Burlington Railroad laid tracks through Billings in 1894, connecting Omaha, Nebraska, with the Northern Pacific, Etta established a roadhouse in the stockyards to cater to the men looking after the herds of cattle and horses shipped through town. Known as Feeley's Place, it was, according to local old-timers, "a bright spot in an otherwise drab and difficult existence." It was a working man's brothel for cow punchers, railroaders, horsemen, and laborers who entered through the doors for a little relief after a long, hard day of work. Hers was a common brothel for common people, whereas the higher-end parlors offered young, beautiful women who could draw high prices from flusher men who could afford their services. Etta's place was devoid of high-end decor; nevertheless, customers could be assured of a good meal, plenty of drink, fine music, and freshly changed sheets. It had a cordial atmosphere, and the men seeking pleasure there could do so without feeling rushed and herded out the door once a transaction was completed.

By the end of 1894, Etta and Walter parted ways, and she married again, this time to an Illinois man named George Lanham. (No evidence suggests that she ever filed for a legal divorce from her previous spouse.) Five years later, the local paper announced her filing for a divorce from Lanham on the grounds of desertion and nonsupport. She also asked to have her birth name, Alice Edwards, restored. According to the announcement, she not only went by the name Etta Feeley, but also Feeley Lanham.

In 1900, the *Red Lodge Picket* reported that "Grandpa Bennett" was going to build "a commodious building" for Miss Etta Feeley in Red Lodge. Could this be the same Mr. Bennett who helped her get her start as an emerging star in Billings? No listings under her name appear in the Red Lodge directories. Perhaps she kept her business on a low profile, or perhaps she thought better of it and opted out of the Red Lodge plan, because Etta eventually headed down to Wyoming to the town of Cody, where city officials granted her a liquor license in 1901. She decided to build a large, two-story house for $4,000 on the 1500 block of Bleistein Avenue, a stretch known as "Crimson Way." While it was under construction, she resided in Garland, thirty miles northeast of Cody, running a brothel that she rented from a madam by the name of Mag Jess. Apparently, her landlord was eager to get her house back, as were Garland town residents. Etta was bombarded with a series of what one local reporter called "petty and malicious litigations." None of those litigations found traction, and she remained in Garland until the construction in Cody was complete in 1902.

The new structure was a high-end bordello, called the White House. With doors ready to open, she sent out invitations to all the men in town for the grand opening event. Local housewives were no doubt incensed when their households received the invites addressed only to their husbands. The note read: "You are respectfully invited to attend the opening of my new residence at Cody, Wyoming, November 1, 1902, Miss Etta Feeley." The business remained in operation well into the 1930s. By then Madam Feeley was an institution in town, and city officials appreciated in their way her contribution to keeping the town's revenue sheets in the pink. Whenever new municipal projects required funding, the town's madams were sure to foot the bill through fines they handed to city officials.

It's not clear whether the successful madam maintained only the Cody house at the time. It's quite possible she had a house back in

Two of Etta's girls mug for the camera on a street corner in front of the madam's house.
PHOTOGRAPH COURTESY OF THE FAY KUHLMAN COLLECTION FROM THE ESTATE OF ALICE EDWARDS LEACH,
PARK COUNTY ARCHIVES, PO2-15-50.

Ferdinand Nevenhuisen, far left, was an alcoholic with a music habit. Etta Feeley ended their marriage over his love affair with the bottle. PHOTOGRAPH COURTESY OF THE FAY KUHLMAN COLLECTION FROM THE ESTATE OF ALICE EDWARDS LEACH, PARK COUNTY ARCHIVES, PO2-15-01.

A Soft Spot for Horses

Feeley's Place was situated on the east side of downtown Billings near the Rimrocks at the end of 4th Avenue North, where the Burlington stockyards were located. Regularly, Etta Feeley watched train cars parked on the secondary tracks that connected the loading docks with the corrals, unloading horses and cattle that had traveled great distances from every corner of the nation. It was an exceptionally long, hard haul for the poor beasts, who would go for extended stretches without food or drink. They would exit the cars, emaciated and weak, to be herded and driven further distances in the harsh climate of central Montana to their awaiting pastures. Etta one time witnessed an entire trainload of cadaverous horses, dehydrated with thirst, gulping up the waters of Alkali Creek. Shortly after, every horse, save one, died, and their bodies were dumped into deep trenches and covered with quicklime. The lone survivor was a tiny colt, the offspring of a blue-gray Percheron draft horse, which one of the local cowhands scooped up and carried over to Etta's place, knowing of the madam's affinity for horses. The colt was in capable hands, as Etta nursed it back to health with warm bottles of milk.

Billings that she rented out for other madams to manage. In any case, love found Etta Feeley once again in 1904, in the form of musician Ferdinand Nevenhuisen, who also went by the name of Fred Nevins. Fred was himself no stranger to the red light district. According to the 1900 Billings census, he was residing—and likely working—in the house of a Norwegian madam, Jennie Bowman, which was sandwiched between Kit Rumley's house and Daisy Duffy's, only a couple doors down from the notorious black madam, Fannie French. Although Etta and Fred exchanged vows in Billings, the two eventually resided just outside of Cody so Etta could manage her house there.

Alas, like many red light musicians of the day, Fred was especially fond of the juice, and his habit took a toll on the couple's marriage. In 1907, Etta filed for a legal separation on grounds of his habitual

Etta and Thomas Leach relax at their stone home in Clarks Fork Canyon, Wyoming, circa 1920. PHOTOGRAPH COURTESY OF THE FAY KUHLMAN COLLECTION FROM THE ESTATE OF ALICE EDWARDS LEACH, PARK COUNTY ARCHIVES, PO2-15-34.

drunkenness. It may have been a bad time for her personal life, but business that year was booming. Cody was pulsing with life as various public works projects were underway—the Wiley Project, the Corbett Tunnel, and the irrigation canals of the Shoshone Project were some of the water developments aimed at hydrating the arid landscape and encouraging farmers to settle in the area. Etta's place was packed night after night with men seeking pleasure and entertainment.

Despite (or perhaps because of) her adventures, Etta Feeley enjoyed a long life. This image was taken in January 1960, when Etta was about ninety, some seven months before her death. PHOTOGRAPH COURTESY OF THE FAY KUHLMAN COLLECTION FROM THE ESTATE OF ALICE EDWARDS LEACH, PARK COUNTY ARCHIVES, PO2-15-22.

All of that came to a screeching halt in the summer of 1908. Funding for the water projects petered out, so Wiley Project management attempted to raise funds with an advertising campaign promising large expanses of land and prosperity to prospective farmers. Special trains brought in hundreds of visitors from back East to take in the sights. Upon arrival, the men simply shook their heads when they saw the sagebrush and salt-sage flats scattered about with unfinished irrigation projects. The campaign fell flat on its face and the project dried up, leaving the creditors to come in and cherry-pick what they could from the rubble to salvage their losses. In the meantime, many workers headed out of town, seeking their fortunes elsewhere.

Etta dusted herself off and was preparing to eke out a living with the population that remained when she was smitten by a man with thick,

A rare glimpse of life outside the brothel shows Etta's employees enjoying an afternoon off, frolicking in a waterfall on the North Fork of the Shoshone River. PHOTOGRAPH COURTESY OF THE FAY KUHLMAN COLLECTION FROM THE ESTATE OF ALICE EDWARDS LEACH, PARK COUNTY ARCHIVES, PO2-15-18.

dark hair and piercing blue eyes. The devastatingly handsome Thomas Leach rendered her heart defenseless, and the two wed in Miles City that very year.

Alas, Mr. Leach was yet another opportunist, an enterpriser who jumped at any chance to make a buck. On their honeymoon, the couple decided to move to Sheridan, Wyoming, where they opened a brothel called the Antler's Bar, which enabled them to build a fortune and amass property throughout Montana and Wyoming.

In 1913, Leach joined forces with a handful of Cody and Sheridan entrepreneurs, forming the Silicone Operating Company to process pure silicone—available in mass quantities just a few miles west of Cody—to market as a scrubbing cleanser. They built a mill and marketed the product, and their efforts met with immediate, astounding success. Meanwhile, Etta was signing over all of her property to her husband, entrusting him with managing the business and finances.

The following year, Thomas traded the Antler for the Old Shaner Place, a 320-acre, turnkey ranch, flush with ninety head of cattle, thirty head of dairy stock, eighteen head of horses, thirty dozen chickens, 140 tons of hay, 7,000 pounds of potatoes, and 700 bushels of "good oats." Leach turned around and put the property up for public auction six months later, to subsequently open a brothel, called the Frisco, in Sheridan.

One of Etta's last appearances in the historical record in those years was in the vice column. In 1915, Etta was convicted for selling liquor to Indians, which was against the law.

By the time the 1930s and early 1940s rolled around, she was back in Billings, living independently, running a "boarding house" on Cook Avenue. Her listing in the 1940 census had her "widowed" and "unable to work." Sometime prior to 1950, Thomas Leach liquidated their accumulated savings of $80,000 and stole away in the middle of the night, leaving Etta penniless, after which she relocated to her humble homestead back on Bennett Creek.

Around 1950, a woman from Cody, who went by the name of Lucretia Adams, ran into Etta—at this point she was back to calling herself Alice—on the prairie up near Clark, Wyoming. Worried about the old woman's ability to care for herself, Lucretia convinced Alice to move back to Cody, and she arranged for the local Mormon church to subsidize Alice's living expenses, renting her a small house and stabling her two horses.

Lucretia purchased three plots at the Riverside Cemetery in Cody: one each for herself and her husband, and one for Alice Leach. Alice died in August 1960 when she was about ninety years old. Her grave remained unmarked until 1976, when Lucretia's daughters arranged to have her name, cowboy boots, and flowers engraved on her headstone, placing it there.

It was a fitting and proper marker for a woman who loved her horses.

OLLIE WARREN—THE BELLE OF BILLINGS

A casket sat open at Smith Funeral Home on a frigid December day, after traveling almost 900 miles from Rochester, Minnesota, to Billings. Now it waited to drop into its final resting place in a mausoleum at the Mountview Cemetery. A small handful of mourners filed in to pay their final respects to the coffin's occupant. Inside the box lay an almost priggish-looking woman garbed in typical Gay Nineties attire.

Ollie Warren combined striking good looks with rare business acumen over a long career as a madam. PHOTOGRAPH COURTESY OF THE MONTANA MEMORY PROJECT, BILLINGS PUBLIC LIBRARY.

Those looking down into the casket probably raised their eyebrows when they saw her, since the year of her death was 1943, not 1895, and her high-necked, brown taffeta dress was about fifty years out of vogue. Other than the dress, the few gamblers and former prostitutes who came to pay their respects would see little indication of the life this seventy-year-old madam had once lived. They would see hardly a vestige of the woman who had once been a diamond-encrusted socialite with a vulgar tongue and a penchant for flaunting her riches throughout Billings. Dressed in velvet riding clothes and wearing her high-plumed hats, she was known for riding side-saddle on her high-stepping horse, a hint of a smile hooked into the corner of her mouth, as she paced before the mansions of the family men who frequented her establishments. Decades after the town had cleared out its thriving red light district, Ollie Warren still appeared stately and subdued, with her brightly hennaed-gray hair and a simple brooch of carved wooden acorns pinned at her throat.

Piecing together Ollie's history from the public record is challenging, as is the case for many women in her profession. She went by various names throughout the years, some of which included Anna O. Dewey, Olive Skerritt, Olive Dewey McDaniels, and Anna Olive McDaniels. The plethora of aliases would be enough to make even the most seasoned researcher or vice squad detective pull out her hair in frustration. In her day, Ollie had been the Belle of Billings, a dark-haired beauty who, according to local old-timers, didn't hesitate to use her stunning looks and aggressive demeanor to get what she wanted. And yet, this professional woman who traded in prostitution among Montana's elite started life as a simple farm girl.

According to the 1880 U.S. Census, Olive Dewey was born in Missouri, the fifth of seven living children to a farming family. Not long after she was born, the Deweys left the Show-Me State and settled in Arapahoe County in Colorado, where Olive spent most of her childhood. Perhaps her feisty disposition was too much to handle for her parents, Jardson and Jane Dewey, because they packed her off to Denver for schooling in a Catholic convent. At seventeen, Ollie married her first husband, Thomas Skerritt. He was an Irish-born horse-trainer, thirteen years her senior, whose family was one of the first to settle in the town of Petersburg (now called Sheridan), also in Arapahoe County. Their union, however, lasted less than two years— they divorced in January 1893 and Skerritt moved back to his family farm to resume training horses. He eventually became a surgical veterinarian in the Denver area. According to city directories, Ollie remained in Denver until 1897. During the final year of her stay there, she is listed as living in "The Row," the city's booming red light district. Her address that year—2005 Market Street—is today a city parking lot, but at the time would have been right on the corner of 20th and Market, which was directly in the heart of a long line of brothels and cribs. In fact, her residence was not more than two doors down from a prostitution house run by one of Denver's most notorious madams of the time, Jennie Rogers.

Throughout this period, Denver was limping back from a major economic depression, which resulted from the nationwide silver bust that panicked everyone in 1893. That financial crash, coupled with a string of harsh winters and years of severe drought, crippled local agriculture. Denver found itself economically strapped. As surrounding silver mine owners shuttered their shafts, unemployed miners fled to the city, looking for work. With the silver-bust closure of major banks and the city now being barraged by unemployed workers, some train companies encouraged people to seek better prospects elsewhere by offering free or reduced one-way fares out of town. In five years' time, the city's population plummeted by 16,000.

This might very well have been the reason that Ollie found herself—a stunning, young, and single woman in a depressed city that had a very high ratio of men to women—resorting to a life on "The Row." As noted throughout the annals of nineteenth-century prostitution, many women found it the only viable way to support themselves. In 1897, she would have been one of at least 1,000 women working that eight-block stretch of The Row on Market Street. In any case, just about the time Denver's economy was beginning to take an upward turn, she made her way to Billings, perhaps to return to a life of virtue. Or, more likely, to take the skills she acquired in Denver to turn a profit and develop a business for herself.

Billings was likely an attractive place for her to settle. It, too, was an agricultural town. Like Arapahoe County, it was set out on the Great Plains. The benchlands along the Yellowstone River were fed by irrigation canals, making it good farming and ranching country. According to a 1982 article in the *Billings Gazette* highlighting the city's centennial, Ollie worked for the prominent madam Etta Feeley. The two had likely known each other in Denver, and the madam very likely would have encouraged Ollie to come work for her in the new agricultural mecca. Inasmuch as she was from a farming family, Ollie probably felt quite at home in her new surroundings.

Upon landing in Billings, the winsome twenty-four-year-old, in addition to working for madam Etta Feeley, took a day job in the dry goods department of the Yegen Brothers Mercantile. She met a prominent local lawyer who found her to be alluring. Although married, he doted over Ollie, showering her with lavish gifts, including glamorous dresses, dazzling gems, and well-bred horses. Notable frontier woman Martha Jane Canary—better known as Calamity Jane—became aware of Ollie's affair with the gentleman. Apparently, Calamity Jane lived in a cabin on Canyon Creek, on the outskirts of town, cutting cedar trees to sell to ranchers for fence posts. She also hauled wood to Billings to sell as firewood for the local residents. According to the story, she drank coffee with the woman of one of the households she delivered to and began asking questions about a familiar face she had occasionally seen wandering about there.

"Who's that man who comes around here once in awhile?" Jane asked the woman, who replied that it was her husband. Jane recognized that man as the very same gentleman who had been cavorting, not so discreetly, on various evenings with Ollie Warren. The same man who had gifted an enormous diamond ring to the young woman. Shortly thereafter, Jane, fully crocked under the influence of her "favorite tipple," headed over to the Yegen Brothers Mercantile, where, according to Dave Conklin's account in *Montana History Weekends: 52 Adventures in History*, she had been previously employed as a clerk, until fired for pulling a knife on one of the customers. This time, she entered the store with a hatchet and confronted Ollie in the dry goods department. Jane staggered toward her intended victim, weapon raised overhead, and threatened "to chop her to pieces then and there." Another clerk easily wrested the hatchet from the drunken woman and escorted her safely out of the building.

Ollie's lawyer companion subsequently financed her first real entrepreneurial endeavor, a grandiose den of iniquity located on

This famous image shows Calamity Jane during the time when she lived in a cabin on Canyon Creek just west of Billings. PHOTOGRAPH COURTESY OF THE MONTANA MEMORY PROJECT, BILLINGS PUBLIC LIBRARY.

the 2500 block of Minnesota Avenue, which she purportedly named after the large diamond ring her paramour had presented her: the Lucky Diamond. It was a white, two-story structure decked in red velvet drapes, lavish furniture, and a large mirrored, mahogany bar.

Love is Blind

Ollie gave her name as Anna O. Dewey on her marriage license with twenty-seven-year-old James McDaniels, and listed her age as thirty-four, a full twelve years younger than her actual age. *PHOTOGRAPH COURTESY OF THE MONTANA MEMORY PROJECT, BILLINGS PUBLIC LIBRARY.*

Madam Ollie Warren was a stunning beauty who was used to getting what she wanted. Take, for example, her acquisition of her brothel, the Lucky Diamond. She was able to convince a prominent lawyer in town to finance her venture. The fact that he was married didn't keep her from encouraging his advances—he showered her with expensive gifts, including the sizable gem that was the namesake for her brothel. According to the Billings Gazette, *when her lover died, Ollie was presumptuous enough to send a large, horseshoe wreath of roses to the house of the grieving family, with a note that read simply, "With love from Olive."*

She was also attracted to young men in the prime of their lives. And it appears that in this domain, she also got what she wanted, albeit underhandedly. As conflicting public records indicate, she may have been a little less than truthful about the actual years behind those youthful good looks. In August 1910, she went to Butte to get hitched with a man from Massachusetts, Harvey Doherty, who recorded his age as thirty-four years on the couple's marriage license. Olive, however, gave her age as thirty on the document, when in actuality she would have been about thirty-seven at the time.

Nine years later, she married again, this time to James McDaniels, who at the time was a sprightly twenty-seven years, in the very bloom of his manhood. While he appears to have had no problem hitching up with the older woman, he may not have realized just how much older his new bride was. Olive stated she was thirty-four years old on the marriage license, when in fact she would have been forty-six at the time—well into middle age.

Ollie set up her home quarters in a back apartment with equally extravagant decor, including a giant crystal chandelier. The other ladies of the house resided upstairs. They were young, gorgeous, and elegantly dressed to entertain.

Out the front stoop, Ollie placed a roadside carriage block—a stepping stone—boldly engraved with her name, so her wealthy patrons and working ladies would not track in mud from the outside. There was no doubt that Ollie had made a name for herself in Billings. But her history in the first decade after the turn of the century proves a bit more elusive.

At one point, she was said to have resided on a ranch in Newcastle, Wyoming, but no records have come to light establishing when that might have occurred. The Lucky Diamond is mentioned in the *Billings Gazette* in 1901 as being under the charge of at least two different women—Fannie Stapleton in April of that year and Della Davidson in June, so it is possible that Ollie leased the brothel while out of town, which was a common enough practice for madams who wanted to keep the income flooding in without having to actually associate themselves too closely with the business. In any event, Ollie was back on record in the *Billings Gazette* with a story in 1902 about an embittered local bartender who intentionally smashed up a buggy belonging to the madam. He landed in jail after he was unable to pay the $200 bond. Then, in 1907, another story reported an incident

To keep her wealthy and well-shod clients from muddying their shoes, Warren placed this stepping stone—engraved with her name—at the front stoop of the Lucky Diamond brothel. PHOTOGRAPH COURTESY OF THE MONTANA MEMORY PROJECT, BILLINGS PUBLIC LIBRARY.

where a local painter issued fraudulent checks around town, three of which were written to Ollie's house. In August 1910, Ollie went to Butte to marry a railroad fireman hailing from Massachusetts, Harvey Doherty. It's unclear where they resided, exactly, but the couple eventually divorced, and Ollie was back at the Lucky Diamond in October 1917 when police raided it.

The city collected $385 in fines that day—an exorbitant amount at the time, in fact the largest fine the city had ever collected—and Ollie's palace of sin was officially shut down. Unfazed, she simply transferred her girls over to Montana Avenue, to a second-floor parlor house between 27th and Broadway, and proceeded to set up shop again. She hired contractors to build an alley access to her new establishment, so she could provide, as she colorfully put it, "a private entry for these stuffed shirts who patronize their churches once a week and my business every night." She later expanded her investments and opened the Virginia Hotel as well.

In 1919, Ollie married yet again, this time to a young firecracker named James McDaniels. The couple relocated to a ranch for a few years on the Crow Reservation near Big Horn where they raised cattle. Theirs was a rocky relationship, as James had numerous run-ins with the law. In July 1927, their marital woes became public when the *Billings Gazette* noted James was arrested for breaking a window at the couple's home and disturbing the peace. He argued that he was trying to retrieve some of his belongings from the residence. Five years later, Ollie filed for divorce on grounds of desertion.

Eventually, Ollie Dewey Warren McDaniels moved to Rochester, Minnesota, to live out her remaining years. In December 1943, nearly fifty years after she began her career in the underground, and well after Billings' red light district had been shut down, she died after suffering for several weeks from a kidney ailment. She took her last train ride back to Billings to be buried in her final resting place.

DUTCH MARY—A KNACK FOR TROUBLE

Mary Burle, (also listed on public record as Marie Burla or Barley) arrived in the United States from Austria around 1875. She was in her early twenties. It's difficult to piece together her trek cross-country to the Montana Territory.

Census and marriage records indicate she had married a laborer, Mathias or Matt Samlin—he was variously recorded as Italian, Yugoslavian, German, and Austrian. It's not clear on which side of the great pond they met, but the couple had their first son, Matt, in 1876. Barely a year later, while residing in Minneapolis, they welcomed their second son, John, into the world. And less than a year after that, their daughter May was born. Their fourth child, Rose, was born two years later. Eventually, the couple must have parted ways or Mathias went the way of all flesh. Mary found herself in Montana alone, with four children to care for and one on the way—from a man whose name no longer appears in the public record. In 1883, Mary landed near Sweeney Creek, just twelve miles west of Helena, when her fifth child arrived. She named her little girl Clara. A single mother of five young children didn't have a lot of options for supporting her family. So Mary did the best she could with the only commodity she had—her body.

It appears she did fairly well for herself working the skin trade. She landed in Miles City, where she was eventually able to open a house of her own. By January 1886, she had established herself as a prominent courtesan, acquiring the moniker of Dutch Mary. But as the public record indicates, Mary's life was far from easy. The successful madam certainly paid some hefty dues throughout her career.

An article in the *Daily Yellowstone Journal* reported that she was accosted by an angry customer, Fred Richards, who broke up her furniture and attempted to beat her. She fled the scene to report the madman to officials. Richards was arrested; unable to pay fines and associated costs, he was "condemned to languish in obscurity in the county jail."

The following month, another story appeared in the *Daily Yellowstone* reporting a drunken soldier from Fort Ellis, decked out in his full uniform with belt, scabbard, and rifle, who started shooting at Mary's house from the outside. He also tried to smash in the door and enter the house. One of the bullets fired right into the building, but, fortunately, no one was injured. He was too drunk to reload his gun before police arrived to arrest him.

Trouble found Dutch Mary yet again when she got into an altercation in her house with a man by the name of Joe Bennet. According to four witnesses, he beat her, so the court fined him $16.90 and let him go. Immediately after the ruling, Mary was called up to the bench to be tried for disturbing the peace because of her fracas with Bennet. She insisted that it was her right to make as much noise as she wished on her own premises, but the court did not agree, fining her $14.70 for her "noisy ways."

Scant evidence of Mary's children exist on the public record. The accounts that do exist, however, reveal a family shaped by their mother's life choices. An 1888 article in the *Daily Yellowstone* reported the arrest of her teenage son, Matt, for swiping some fruit from a street stand. He died six months later from neuralgia of the heart. All three of her daughters followed in their mother's footsteps with careers in the night trade. Her son John, however, tried to make an honest living at one point as a ranch hand.

Sometime between 1888 and 1899, Dutch Mary moved to Billings. In April 1899, the *Billings Gazette* reported that her daughter May, a prostitute from a southside resort in town, died of pneumonia. Five months later, Mary built a two-story house on Minnesota Avenue, next door to Ollie Warren's Lucky Diamond, and just two doors down from the prominent black madam, Fannie French. A saloon occupied the downstairs, while Dutch Mary's women worked in the upper-level rooms.

One Saturday in January 1902, the madam hosted a dance at a southside theater, Tivoli Hall, where she hired a prominent star, La Belle Quigley, to perform that night with the other ladies of her house. The dance went late into the evening, and Quigley begged Mary to call the night to an end. The madam refused, and a fight ensued. Dutch Mary testified in court that the "prima donna" pulled a knife on the madam and proceeded to "cut a large chunk out of her neck." Miss Quigley was subsequently charged with second degree assault.

Dutch Mary apparently recovered from the wound, only to run into trouble again in October of that same year after a couple of firebugs went on a spree in the resort district over the course of a week. Mary's house was the seventh house hit in seven days. As the flames raged, a bystander, Chas Burton, overheard a man tell another, "In about an hour from now, we can have a bigger blaze than this, and hay burns much faster." Later that evening, a saloon keeper down the street, William Bennett, overheard a man sitting at the bar who was talking about setting fire to a livery stable. Burton and Bennett reported what they'd witnessed to the police and local livery stables;

The Revolving C Note

Across the street from Dutch Mary's bordello on 24th and Mendenhall Avenue, her daughter Clara kept a cathouse of her own. She was arrested on Thanksgiving Day 1905, not only for keeping a house of disorder, but for "practicing hypnotism" on a man and "rendering him defenseless against her." According to an article in the Billings Gazette, she "enchanted" the man, having him so completely "under her spell" that he lost "all sense of respect for himself or members of his family" and became "bent on marrying her." Despite multiple warnings to keep her "hands off" the man, Clara continued to see him. The police apparently had enough evidence stacked against her for such strange accusations and set bail at $100. When she appeared in court, she pled guilty, and the court fined her another $100. Indignant at the fee they demanded, she refused to pay, so was "sent below" for fifty days (at which time the court returned her bail money to her). Finally, at wit's end from being held in captivity in a dark cell for so long, she conceded and went upstairs to pay the chief. She reached into her undergarments and pulled out the same $100 she had used to pay bail.

guards stood station in all the barns throughout the night. An army of business and resort owners along Minnesota Avenue put men on watch on their properties as well. Finally, around midnight, a suspect who was loitering in the alleys of the red light district was arrested. He had been a visitor in town for several weeks, and the police reported that he was "partially demented." He was taken down to the station to get "sweated" for information.

In her line of work, Dutch Mary no doubt ran into her share of opportunists, but one in particular bit off more than he could chew. A man traveling through Billings on his way to Red Lodge came into Mary's place and bought a bottle of beer with the last coins in his pocket. He chatted up the madam, and the two seemed to hit it off well. His eyes about popped out of his head when he looked at the load of diamond rings Mary wore on her fingers. He asked for a closer look and she obliged. He bent over her hand, then proceeded to bite one of the jewels in an attempt to break it free from its setting. Mary was too strong for his grip and was able to pull away before he could free and swallow the gemstone.

Poor Mary seemed to be a target for trouble, but in January 1903 she set herself up for more than she had ever bargained for. She was forty-two when she married a handsome twenty-seven-year-old baseball star named Frank Tobin.

Frank hailed from New Haven, Connecticut, and thanks to his athletic prowess had risen to hero status soon after he joined the Billings semi-professional ball club. But only three months into his baseball contract, he was convicted of attempted assault on a ten-year-old girl. Stumbling along the sidewalk one afternoon, he came across the daughter of a local barber and proceeded to follow her for several blocks, terrifying her with his indecent advances until she screamed for help. Police found him staggering in an alley behind a saloon and immediately arrested him.

It was shortly after that incident that Frank connected with Dutch Mary, and within the year the lovebirds shared their vows.

Although the start of their marriage appeared peaceful to anyone on the outside, the illusory honeymoon didn't last long. Frank's true colors emerged, and calling theirs a rocky union would be a gross understatement. Dutch Mary found herself stuck in a hopeless situation with a man who was a mean drunk with serious anger management issues.

A mere two months into their marriage, a fire broke out in Mary's brothel on the corner of Minnesota Avenue and 24th Street. It had just suffered a fire five days prior. According to a dispatch article in the *Anaconda Standard,* this was at least the fifth time Dutch Mary's house had been torched. The firemen were timely in arriving at the scene, but the arsonist had dumped oil to fuel the fire, and water pressure was low. The row of buildings on either side were saved with great difficulty, but Mary's house was completely destroyed. Unfortunately, her insurance policy had been cancelled due to previous conflagrations. Frank didn't help matters much when he tried to interfere with the firefighters as they worked to extinguish the blaze. He spent the night in the bullpen and faced fines the next morning.

Mary's brothels weren't the only ones to take multiple beatings. She was victim to a great number of drubbings herself. Time and time again, reports emerged in the local papers about Frank getting locked up for assaulting his wife. He "refused to work on the streets" and "lived on bread and water." One time he threatened Mary with arson. Soon after, she again found her house filled with smoke, and a bed on the downstairs level was destroyed by flames. The fire did little actual damage, but the soaking it took to extinguish the blaze nearly ruined her property. Mary knew her husband had set the fire, but she lacked the proof to convict him. Her patience was running thin.

Frank soon found himself behind bars for ninety days, with a $250 fine, for laying his wife's scalp open with a large spittoon, chopping up her piano, and breaking furniture in her establishment. Once released, Frank appeared to sober up, and Dutch Mary decided to give him yet another chance.

In 1905, she opened the doors to her new brothel, the Star, on the corner of 25th and Minnesota Avenue. Her husband had been dry for nearly two months, so, giving him the benefit of the doubt, she put him to work behind the bar.

That was a big mistake. With a superabundance of booze under his charge, how could an alcoholic resist the temptation? Frank inevitably started sipping on the job, and that's when the trouble began. Again. Someone may have looked at him funny, Mary may have made a snarky remark about his falling off the wagon—who knows? But something rubbed him the wrong way, whipping him into a fury and causing him to destroy everything in his path. And that path, once again, led Frank straight to the slammer.

He managed to shatter the large, decorative mirror that hung at the back of the bar. All the glassware, demijohns, and furniture were annihilated. Frank beat Dutch Mary to a pulp before he fled the scene. Police nabbed him as he attempted to leap onto the rear end of a passenger train pulling out of the train yard. They threw him into the brig to dry out, but Frank was in a mood and hardly done with his tirade. Left alone in his cell, according to a *Billings Gazette* account, "he climbed on top of the cages, tore out the electric wiring, wrenched the water pipes awry, and kicked and tore out a patch of the lathed and plastered ceiling, about 6 feet square." When police returned to find the mess, they handcuffed their prisoner, removed his shoes, and threw him into a darkened cell. In the past, likely because of his hero baseball status, he had gotten away with kicking out all the window panes of one of his jail cells with no charges pressed. Officials had chalked it up as a one-time deal. This time, however, Frank was spanked with a felony—a maximum punishment of five years, along with a $2,000 fine.

Even with her husband locked away for an extended sentence, Dutch Mary still ran into troubles that got her name printed in the local papers. In July 1907, the Little Terrace Saloon opened a new addition: a wine room. Dutch Mary was one of the few women who frequented the little room adjoining the back of the bar. Because women were prohibited from being served in such places, the bartender was arrested for serving Mary drinks.

A bigger story appeared in the paper just three months later, when eleven sugar factory employees were enjoying a night of gambling at the Star. According to the *Billings Gazette*, a disgruntled rancher, sore from losing, left the game and promptly reported to the police that he had been fleeced. Two officers immediately executed a raid. One kept guard at the back door while the other entered the front. The gamblers were seated in a circle on the floor, coats off, and were so engrossed in their game of craps that they never looked up to see the officer enter the room. The bluecoat reportedly saw the dice, saw the cash, and promptly arrested the lot of them, collecting what money they had—$177—for bail money. According to this first account, the men tossed the dice while en route to the police station, so officers were left to "look for the bones" in an effort to collect the damning evidence. A follow-up article four days later in the same paper changed the story, pointing the finger at Dutch Mary for thwarting the men's imprisonment. In this version, the madam had warned the men of the officers' arrival, enabling the group to hide their stash and toss the dice. Luckily for Mary, the rancher who had filed the initial complaint failed to show up in court to testify, so the case was dismissed.

Law enforcement has always been a dangerous job. Billings police officer Enos Nelson, seated at far right, was shot and killed on December 6, 1917, at the Little Terrace Saloon while responding to a report of a man with a gun in the bar. PHOTOGRAPH COURTESY OF THE MONTANA MEMORY PROJECT, BILLINGS PUBLIC LIBRARY, BPL2013.01.005.

During this period, Dutch Mary had been buying up properties in Stillwater County, one of which included a "resort" in Columbus. In July 1908, Frank got out on early release. Apparently, Mary had it in her heart to forgive the man she loved. But alas, once again, her tumultuous family affairs wound up in the local papers. The couple had traveled to Columbus to visit the madam's new brothel. As before, things spiraled out of control when Frank's temper got the best of him, and he managed to smash a collection of furniture and break out several windows of the bordello before throwing his wife's travel bag into the Yellowstone River. He subsequently found himself locked up for another three months for disturbing the peace and assaulting his wife.

Mary finally gathered enough moxie to divorce the man who had caused her so much injury and strife. By 1910, she was a single woman again. After that, she seems to have avoided much negative publicity, and continued running her brothel and prospering well into the 1930s as one of Billings' wealthiest citizens. Meanwhile, according to the 1930 federal census, Frank somehow wound up in Walla Walla, Washington, languishing in the state penitentiary and spending his time working as a commissary cook.

In 1938, hard times hit again. Mary's daughter Clara succumbed that July to an illness that had afflicted her for two years. Dutch Mary seemed to give up once she lost her daughter. Three months later, she transferred all of her properties to her son John, and by November, the eighty-two-year-old madam was dead.

7

$\mathcal{B}ozeman$
A Hotbed of Vice

Like every other community in Montana, Bozeman had a vibrant red light district. It was situated along the alley behind Main Street, between Main and Mendenhall, running east to west from Bozeman Avenue to Rouse Avenue.

And as in every other red light district in Montana, the women who worked there left little historical trace behind, except in the police blotters whenever the local fathers decided to send the police in to "clean up" the town. In 1898, for example, Bozeman mayor J. V. Bogert enacted Ordinance 173, designed to suppress prostitution. A related decree, Ordinance 188, made vagrancy a crime and specifically singled out women who might behave in "any immodest, drunken, profane or obscene manner." Naturally, the world's oldest profession cannot simply be legislated away, and before long, the Bozeman tenderloin was up and running again. The erection of a Carnegie Library on North Bozeman, however, directly across the street from known brothels and several Chinese businesses, prompted another backlash. In the early twentieth century, the Women's Christian Temperance Union urged the police to crack down, and in 1910, fines for women running brothels ranged from $10 to $25. In 1911, Bozeman's chief of police reported to a city council meeting that "[b]efore closing the red light district arrests averaged 86 per month, after closing arrests averaged 22," indicating that the suppression efforts were rather successful. So much so that by 1917, with Montana attorney general Sam Ford's effort to completely eradicate prostitution from the state underway, there was almost no work to be done in Bozeman.

Prior to Ford's campaign in 1917, prostitutes and madams were alternately tolerated and persecuted in a cycle of arrests and fines common to many communities. The *Anaconda Standard* of January 4, 1896, contains a feature article detailing Bozeman's attempts to control the flesh trade. As usual, the "unfortunates" were harassed with routine $5 fines, under Ordinance 85. The more serious the attempt to eliminate the vice, the higher the fines would climb, on the presumption that if the penalty were stiff enough, the madams would have to leave Bozeman and set up shop elsewhere. Similarly, a notice from an 1887 newspaper suggested that the real culprit was alcohol. "Put a higher license upon those who keep liquor for sale at a house of prostitution and you will have taken a step toward morality," the writer urged.

This interaction with the legal system affords one of the few ways to track madams through history—their almost routine appearance in local arrest records. Dia Johnson, a Bozeman disc jockey who has taken an interest in digging through old records to reveal Bozeman's red light history, has discovered a trove of such records while researching the Bozeman Police Department. She found that Bozeman court records from a single year during the 1880s listed more than 600 prostitutes and madams. By 1905, however, the same source shows only 189 women working in the profession. In an interview with Bozeman's KBZK Channel 4 news, Johnson said, "Looking through old books and records and court minutes, I just found that these women kept appearing and yet there was nothing ever written about them in the paper until their deaths. They had incredible land holdings and made so much money I knew there was a story to tell for these women."

While copper kings and railroad barons sent most of their Montana-made wealth to California, New York, and elsewhere, madams tended to spread their largesse closer to home. An example of this involves Bozeman's Carnegie Library, which was constructed in 1903 on city-donated land—directly across the street from the opium dens of Chinatown and the brothels and cribs of the red light district. Reformers chose that location for the specific purpose of clearing out the disreputable neighborhood, which did, in fact, wither once the library opened. Ironically, it was the philanthropy of local madams that filled the library's shelves with books.

BIG LOU—
A CULTIVATOR IN THE VALLEY OF FLOWERS

Big Lou arrived in Bozeman in 1873 with money to spend. Heaps of money. She had just arrived from Helena, where her entrepreneurial sensibilities placed her as one of the preeminent property barons of the red light.

Louisa Couselle (aka Louise, with the last name Courselle, Cassell, and Cousell) hailed from England and grew up well-educated in Brooklyn, New York. When she was a teen, she and her cousin headed to Nevada, where she appeared in Nevada's 1865 tax assessment list as a "Retail Dealer in Liquor." She then headed to Helena via Missoula, to cultivate her prostitution empire, amassing properties and financing loans to fellow community members.

One Sunday afternoon in Helena, during the fall of 1869, the bells at the Catholic Church and school on Rodney Street rang out an alarm. Hundreds of people rushed to the scene to witness the Helena Theatre burning down. A theatrical group had just arrived from San Francisco and was in the dressing room, preparing for the evening's performance, when the fire ignited there. The famous composer and violinist, Paul Louis Boulon, was also in the room. Since the structure was built of highly combustible materials, flames soon spread out of control, overtaking the entire building and spreading to adjacent buildings on the east and south sides. Stage sets and props, wardrobes, and musical instruments were completely consumed by the flames. Boulon was critically burned while trying to save his sheet music and coveted violin.

The New North-West paper out of Deer Lodge reported that the "wind was blowing a hurricane" through town, and eight or nine Wood Street "houses"—none of which contained actual families—were lost to the inferno. Names of proprietresses suffering property losses included a Kate Smith, Mrs. Zipp, Kate Buchanan, and Mrs. Kelly. The Kan-Kan, the Kiyus, and the Senate were some of the district's businesses that reported significant damage as well. Residents of every building on Wood Street below and across from the Boulder block had emptied out their premises as well as they could to avoid the flames.

One proprietress, known locally on a first-name basis as Vivion, had an old stone house that slowed the blaze's progression toward the heart of downtown. Citizens frantically tore down wooden-framed buildings on Bridge Street just before the fire engulfed them, which helped slow the spread. These efforts plus the good fortune of the wind blowing in a favorable direction saved the city of Helena from complete destruction. Big Lou's two-story Helena brothel, the Bon Ton, however, took a hard hit when the fire blew through, suffering $3,000 in damages. Lou was able to repair the damages and open her doors for business once again.

Unlike some of the other heavy players in Helena's demimonde, Big Lou wasn't mean-spirited in her pursuit of wealth. She was more interested in building a community of friendly competition while making keen investments. She helped other women seeking self-efficacy to get established in the business—such as Fannie Spencer—and was known to be generous in extending sliding-scale loans and mortgages to fellow members of the community. To poor families, she charged a 2.5 percent annual interest rate, members of the middle class 2.5 percent per month, and those from the higher echelons 2.5 percent interest per day.

Helena's red light empire had been thriving, and a handful of madams were ruthlessly vying for power and position. For example, Chicago Joe joined forces with madam Lillie McGraw and proprietress Delores Jarra by signing a court petition to have a fellow proprietress, Mary Kelly, institutionalized for insanity. Fortunately for Kelly, the courts found no basis for the claim and determined the other madams were trying to defraud Kelly of her assets. Competition was getting fierce.

The tipping point for Lou's Helena stay came in January 1874, when the Bon Ton took another hit, this time by a blaze sparked in the Chinese district. Lou's establishment suffered $2,000 in damages, while other madams—Nellie Perkins and Mollie Grahm—saw all their assets reduced to cinders. Proprietor-prostitutes choked on nearly $12,000 in total damages, with the city suffering more than $1 million in losses overall. Perhaps that was the signal to Big Lou that it was time to move on, because eight months later she sold the scorched lot where the Bon Ton once stood to Chicago Joe, for a meager $150, and headed to Bozeman—the Valley of the Flowers. Men were plentiful there—ranch hands and soldiers from Fort Ellis, which was six miles east of town, were hungry for the company of women—and, aside from the Chinese houses open for business, Lou would find little to no competition from other proprietor-prostitutes.

Upon landing in the eight-year-old town with cash in hand, Big Lou scooped up a whopping fifteen properties between Main Street and Mendenhall from Bozeman to Rouse Avenues. She was so successful that within two years' time she was able to buy two farms outside of town. In terms of wealth, she was in the top five percent of the local population. She helped lay the foundation for a thriving red light district, again playing mentor when she helped a young woman by the name of Kitty Warren get a strong foothold in the burgeoning district. By 1878, Big Lou was noted as one of the fifty-nine "heavy taxpayers of Gallatin County" in the *Avant Courier Annual Almanac*.

The end for Big Lou came in June 1886 when she died of dropsy at the age of fifty-four, which was likely the result of heavy drinking combined with the taking of too many drugs—laudanum, mercury, opium, and pain killers. When she passed, she left behind an estate worth $20,000, which would be nearly $500,000 in today's dollars. According to the Brooklyn, New York, directory of 1884, she had a residence there and was widowed to a James Couselle. A 2015 article in the *Bozeman Daily Chronicle* reported it was a five-story mansion that the madam willed to her daughter. Probate records indicate her daughter's name was Harriett Whittaker. Lou's body was shipped back to Brooklyn to be buried in Green-Wood Cemetery.

Louisa Couselle's obituary read, "It is not necessary for us to describe her calling, or occupation, but that she was a remarkable women in many respects cannot and will not be gainsaid by anyone who knew her."

KITTY WARREN AND FRANKIE BUTTNER— KIN SPIRITS

Two prominent Bozeman madams were Roberta Warn and Louise Buttner, better known as Kitty Warren and Frankie Buttner, respectively. Not only did they share an address in Bozeman's red light district, they shared the close bond of family—they were sisters.

Frankie had a house that still stands today, in an alley behind Main Street, between Bozeman and Rouse Avenues. The ladies of the house would stand in the doorways, cat-calling to the men strolling by outside. Madam Buttner got her start on the stage, performing for adoring crowds in the vaudeville circuit. She took a break from her career and married a saloon keeper, but eventually left him to return to Bozeman's demimonde. An article in Bozeman's paper stated she had been a "leading footlight favorite," and speculated, "Why she abandoned the stage and adopted her sinful and downward career is unknown, but it is more likely the old, old story of a woman's trusting innocence and man's perfidy."

Apparently that "trusting innocence" didn't have too much of an effect on her business dealings. One evening, Frankie confronted two Chinese tenants who resided in her house. They had failed to make good on their rent money, so she confronted them with a pearl-handled Colt revolver in the alley and proceeded to blow a hole through one of them.

She was just twenty-one years old when she went through a lengthy trial over the alley incident. She was convicted, but to avoid her sentencing, she took some poison and chased it with a few swigs from a whiskey bottle. According to an article in the *Avant Courier*, a man found her splayed out on a lounge chair, and she told him that "in less than six hours" she "would be a corpse." Her sister was devastated when she discovered Frankie had died.

Kitty—who also went by the nicknames of Katie and Burtie among her close circle of friends—had previously been a milliner and had a millinery on Main Street, across the street from Big Lou's milliner shop. Many young women who found themselves at the bottom of the labor force—as servants, seamstresses, chambermaids, tailors, or milliners—wound up getting siphoned off into the sex industry, especially when they found themselves alone, fending for themselves. Often, they worked the sex trade under the pretense of running milliner or seamstress shops.

According to Bozeman-based Dia Johnson, a researcher interested in local madams, Kitty married a prospector by the name of John Warn. "He was a man trying to make a buck," says Johnson. He went to Billings, then Miles City, and kept traveling as far as he could get." Kitty was granted a divorce based on abandonment, after which she started turning tricks. She began working for Big Lou, who eventually became her mentor, loaning her funds in 1875 to purchase properties and help expand Bozeman's red light district. Kitty had a lavish bordello on Mendenhall that had seven bedrooms, each with a wood stove, mirror, and brass bed.

In 1885, less than two years after her sister committed suicide, Kitty attempted to light a cigar from an oil lamp. She may have been doped up on drink or some other substance, and might have avoided sparking the fire had she been sober. As it were, the lamp's oil spilled all over her dress, and the madam suffered terrible injuries when the fabric ignited and engulfed her in flames. The twenty-five year old languished in excruciating pain for a month before finally succumbing to her injuries. According to an 1885 article in the *Bozeman Weekly Chronicle*, a Mandan man from South Dakota, who was a former husband, came to town to grieve and pay his respects before she died.

Bozeman's soiled doves worked together to wrap up Kitty's post-mortem affairs. A woman named Fanny Wood washed Kitty's body to prepare it for burial as well as took inventory of the madam's house to prepare for the public auction of her estate. Kitty's mentor and close friend, Big Lou, paid $10 to have a grave dug next to Kitty's sister, Frankie, on whose headstone Kitty had inscribed, "Farewell O Sister dear, farewell, Thou has left me in this lonely world of pain, Oh, may we meet in Heavenly bliss to dwell."

Morality Play

Mrs. Warren's Profession *sat on his desk for eight years before Irish-born playwright George Bernard Shaw actually got to see his play publicly performed on a London stage in 1902. Critics tore it to pieces, and it was banned from the stage for its forthright social commentary—namely, dealing with prostitution, morality, and upper-class hypocrisies.*

The play features a successful madam named Kitty Warren. According to Dia Johnson, an expert on Bozeman madams, the use of Kitty Warren's name is no accident. Apparently, an actress friend of the playwright convinced the author to pen the piece after she had visited Montana.

When actors performed the show in a New York theater in 1905, police rushed the stage and arrested the entire cast and crew for allegedly violating state obscenity laws. By today's standards, the script contains nothing obscene, but in its day audiences squirmed when forced to face some dark truths. The play is not so much about prostitution, per se, as it is about the hypocrisy of morality— where promiscuous women are condemned without having other feasible means of self-support. "Decency is indecency's conspiracy of silence," Shaw noted in his "Author's Apology," which he wrote after his work finally made the public stage. He claimed to have written the play for women, stating that it was performed and produced mainly through the determination of women who realized the timeliness and power of the lessons put forth in the play.

$\mathscr{Sources}$

Most of the historical newspaper articles listed here can be read online at Chronicling America: Historic American Newspapers, a digital archive of the Library of Congress, at chroniclingamerica.loc.gov. In addition, several books and articles provided context and general information for multiple chapters. These include:

Baumler, Ellen. "Justice as an Afterthought: Women and the Montana Prison System." *Montana: The Magazine of Western History,* Vol. 58, No. 2 (Summer 2008), Montana Historical Society; "Soiled Doves: Life on Helena's Tenderloin." *More from the Quarries of Last Chance Gulch.* Online.

MacKell, Jan. *Red Light Women of the Rocky Mountains.* University of New Mexico Press, Albuquerque, 2009.

Morgan, Lael. *Wanton West: Madams, Money, Murder and the Wild Women of Montana's Frontier.* Chicago Review Press, Chicago, 2011.

Peavy, Linda, and Ursula Smith. *Pioneer Women: The Lives of Women on the Frontier.* Smithmark, New York, 1996.

Rutter, Michael. *Boudoirs to Brothels: The Intimate World of Wild West Women.* Farcountry Press, Helena, 2014; *Upstairs Girls: Prostitution in the American West.* Farcountry Press, Helena, 2005.

Strahn, Derek. "Tycoons in Petticoats: Frontier Montana's Uncommon Red Light Madams." *Distinctly Montana.* July 7, 2006.

Trumbull, Jonathan (editor). *Prostitution.* K. G. Saur Verlag GmbH & Co., Munich, 1993.

Mothers of Vice—Making a House a Home

Barry, Kathleen L. *The Prostitution of Sexuality.* New York University Press, New York, 1995.

Department of Agriculture, Labor, and Industry, State of Montana. *Federal Writers' Project: Montana: A State Guide Book.* Hastings House, Montana, 1949.

Gilfoyle, Timothy J. "Archaeologists in the Brothel: 'Sin City,' Historical Archaeology and Prostitution." *Historical Archaeology.* Society for Historical Archaeology, Rockville, MD, 2005. 39(1): pp. 133-141.

Martin, Cy. *Whiskey and Wild Women: An Amusing Account of the Saloons and Bawds of the Old West.* Hart Publishing, New York, 1974.

Montana Historical Society Officers and Members. *Contributions to the Historical Society of Montana with its Transactions, Act of Incorporation, Constitution, Ordinances, Vol. II.* State Publishing Company, Helena, 1896.

Montana Historical Society Staff. *Not in Precious Metals Alone: A Manuscript History of Montana.* Montana Historical Society Press, Helena, 1976.

Parrett, Aaron. *Montana Then and Now.* Bangtail Press, Bozeman, MT, April 1, 2014.

Chapter 1: Pioneering Petticoats—The Madams of Bannack and Virginia City

Allen, Frederick. *A Decent Orderly Lynching: The Montana Vigilantes.* Carto's Library, 2004.

Anaconda Standard (Anaconda, MT). June 20, 21, 1891; March 31, 1891; December 20, 1897; "In Society," July 23, 1899; and November 7, 1899.

Bancroft, Hubert Howe. *History of the Pacific States of North America: Washington, Idaho, and Montana 1845-1889.* The History Company, San Francisco, 1890; and *The Works of Hubert Howe Bancroft: History of British Columbia. 1887.* The History Company, San Francisco, 1887.

Benton Weekly Record (Benton, MT). "A Valiant Official," August 18, 1883; also September 15, 1883.

Blair, Madeleine. *Madeleine: An Autobiography.* Harper & Brothers, New York and London, 1919. Introduction by Judge Ben B. Lindsey.

Butler, Anne M. *Gendered Justice in the American West: Women Prisoners in Men's Penitentiaries.* University of Illinois Press, Champaign, IL, August 1, 1999.

Butte Inter Mountain (Butte, MT). March 22, 1902; December 22, 23, 1903.

Culberson, William C. *Vigilantism: Political History of Private Power in America.* Greenwood Press, Westport, CT, 1990.

The Daily Missoulian (Missoula, MT). November 15, 1914.

Dimsdale, Thomas. *The Vigilantes of Montana: A Full and Complete History of the Chase, Capture, Trial and Execution of All the Outlaws Who Figured in the Bloody Drama.* University of Oklahoma Press, Norman, OK, 1953.

East Oregonian (Pendleton, OR). September 23, 1913.

Forney, Gary R. *Discovery Men: The Fairweather Party and Montana's El Dorado.* Xlibris Corp., 2009.

Frazier, Ian. *Great Plains.* Picador Press, New York, 1989.

Gilfoyle, Timothy J. "Archaeologists in the Brothel: 'Sin City,' Historical Archaeology and Prostitution." *Historical Archaeology.* Society for Historical Archaeology, Rockville, MD, 2005. 39(1): pp. 133-141.

Hereford, Robert A. *Old Man River: The Memories of Captain Louis Rosche, Pioneer Steamboatman.* The Caxton Printers Ltd., Caldwell, ID, 1942, pp. 105, 200, 204-233.

Hogg, Sara Marie. "The Strange Saga of Madame Mustache." Venture Galleries. November 24, 2014.

Johnson, Randall A. "The Mullan Road: A Real Northwest Passage." *The Pacific Northwesterner,* Vol. 39, No. 2, 1995. Online reprint: historylink.org.

Knauber, Al. "Retracing the Mullan Road: A Once-Vital Route across the Continental Divide." *Independent Record* (Helena, MT). August 24, 2014.

Lepley, John G. *The Madame and the Four Johns: Fort Benton's Lawless Years of Gold, Whiskey and Hostiles.* Self-published, 2013.

Madisonian (Virginia City, MT). October 5, 1895; "Virginia City Brothel Subject of Presentation in Bozeman," August 22, 2012.

Malone, Michael P., et al. *Montana: A History of Two Centuries.* University of Washington Press, Seattle, 1991.

Mather, R. E., and R. E. Boswell. "Henry Plummer." *Wild West,* August 1993.

Miller, Donald C. *Ghost Towns of Montana.* TwoDot, Helena, 2008.

Montana Department of Environmental Quality. "A Guide to Abandoned Mine Reclamation." deq.mt.gov

Montana Historical Society Staff. *Not in Precious Metals Alone: A Manuscript History of Montana.* Montana Historical Society Press, Helena, 1976.

Montana Post (Virginia City, MT). "Discovery and Settlement of Alder Creek," January 21, 1865, p. 2.; "Returned," April 20, 1867, p. 8; "An Opiate," May 25, 1867, p. 8; May 14, 1869.

Nash, Jay Robert. *Encyclopedia of Western Lawmen & Outlaws.* Rowman & Littlefield, Lanham, MD, 1989.

Ovitt, Mable. *Golden Treasure.* Self-published, 1954.

Philipsburg Mail (Philipsburg, MT). June 22, 1893.

River Press (Fort Benton, MT). April 6, 1904.

Truth (Salt Lake City). March 28, 1908.

Virginia City, Montana Chamber of Commerce. "A Brief City History and the Virginia City Preservation Alliance." Virginiacity.com.

Waits, Susan. *Historical Inventory of the Marysville Ghost Town.* U.S. Bureau of Land Management, Missoula.

Walker-Kuntz, Sunday, et al. "Historical Background and Significance of Garnet Ghost Town." *National Register of Historic Places Nomination of 2009.* U.S. Bureau of Land Management, Missoula.

Walsh, William, and William Orem. *Biennial Report of the Inspector of Mines of the State of Montana for the Years 1907-8.* Independent Publishing Company, Helena, 1908.

Web, Jaci. "Virginia City Brothel Days." *Billings Gazette* (Billings, MT). June 29, 2014.

Weed, Walter Harvey. *The Mines Handbook, Succeeding the Copper Handbook: Describing the Mining Companies of the World. Vol. 15.* The Mines Handbook Co., Tuckahoe, NY, 1922.

Weekly Miner (Butte, MT). September 23, 1879.

Weiser, Kathy. *Legends of America.* "Leading Madams of the Old West," December 2012; "Painted Ladies," December 2013; "Legends of Montana: Bannack, Montana," April 2015.

Weiss, Gillian. *French Historical Studies,* Vol. 28, No. 2 (Spring 2005), Society for French Historical Studies.

Chapter 2: Helena—A City of Capital Delights

Agnew, Jeremy. *Medicine in the Old West: A History, 1850-1900.* McFarland, Jefferson, NC, 2010.

Anaconda Standard (Anaconda, MT). August 7, 1893; "Came West to Win: Career of A Woman Once the Wife of A Chicago Alderman—Robbed of Her Jewels," June 11, 1896; "'Chicago Joe' Dead," October 26, 1899; "A Will Contest: A War Fight Will Be Put Up for A Disreputable Woman's Estate," April 12, 1901, p. 10.

Ancestry.com. Mike Bittrick (Toppo Bittrick family).

Baird, Kennon. "The Red Light District: Madams Josephine 'Chicago Jo' Hensley and Belle 'Crazy Belle' Crafton." Also "Dorothy's Rooms—19½ South Main." *Helena As She Was: An Open History Resource for Montana's Capital City.* helenahistory.org.

Bancroft, Hubert Howe. *History of the Pacific States of North America: Washington, Idaho, and Montana 1845-1889.* The History Company, San Francisco, 1890.

Barry, Kathleen L. *The Prostitution of Sexuality.* New York University Press, New York, 1995.

Baumler, Ellen. "Dorothy's Rooms: Helena's Last, and Some Say Best, Place." *Montana Women Writers: A Geography of the Heart.* Ed. Caroline Patterson. Farcountry Press, Helena, 2006. p. 310; *Montana Moments: History on the Go.* Montana Historical Society Press, Helena, 2010; *Montana Moments Blog.* "Chicago Joe." January 9, 2012.

Baumler, Ellen and Christy Goll. "Wicked, Wild, and Wonderful History." *406 Woman,* Vol. 5. Skirts Publishing, Whitefish, MT. June/July 2012, p. 20.

Bazaar, Susan. Personal phone interview. December 10, 2014.

Bowsher, Kim. "A History of Violence: Ogden's 25th Street." *Utah Stories.* August 29, 2014.

Brier, Warren J. "Tilting Skirts and Hurdy-Gurdies: A Commentary on Gold Camp Women." *Montana: The Magazine of Western History,* Vol. 19, No. 4 (Autumn 1960).

Butler, Anne Katherine M. *The Tarnished Frontier: Prostitution in the Trans-Mississippi West, 1865-1890.* Dissertation for the University of Maryland. University Microfilms International, Ann Arbor, 1979.

Butte Semi-Weekly Miner (Butte, MT). January 22, 1887; July 2, 1887.

Corrigan, Terence. "The Seedy Side of Helena." *Independent Record* (Helena, MT). August 24, 2014.

Emeigh, John Grant. "Deadly Disaster: Firefighters, Onlookers Perish in 1895 Explosion." *The Montana Standard* (Butte, MT). August 13, 2012.

Freeman, Paul. "Big Dorothy Becomes Legend." *Daily Inter Lake* (Kalispell, MT). May 16, 1973.

Frisk, Trudy. "Lilacs and Rhubarb—Signs of the Settlers." *Cowboylife.* Interactive Broadcasting Corporation, 2015.

Graña, Marie. *Pioneer Doctor: The Story of a Woman's Work.* TwoDot, Helena, 2005.

Great Falls Tribune (Great Falls, MT). August 8, 1888.

"The Hankins." *Chicago Tribune* (Chicago, IL). February 14, 1875, p. 3.

Helena City Directory, 1868.

Helena Independent (Helena, MT). December 22, 1881; May 19, 1883; May 8, 11, 1884; "Night Workers," June 21, 1889; May 21, 1890; December 13, 1890; November 29, 1891; January 23, 1930, p. 2.

Helena Weekly Herald (Helena, MT). July 31, 1873; September 9, 1880; May 24, 1883, p. 7; "Opening Night: Dedication Last Night of the Helena Roller Skating Amphitheatre," May 31, 1883, p. 8; "Preparations for Beecher in Helena on August 15," July 26, 1883, p. 2; May 15, 1884; October 23, 1884; February 17, 1887.

"The History of Helena, Montana." BigSkyFishing.com: Your Online Source for Montana Fishing Information. 2002-2011.

Independent Record (Helena, MT). "Thank You," April 29, 1925; February 18, 1925; "No. 23175 Summons," April 3, 1952; July 31, 1964; "Is Dorothy Baker Still in Business?" March 26, 1970; "Injunction Issued in Health Case," September 20, 1970; "No Complaints About Dorothy's Says County Attorney Dowling," October 4, 1972; "Mad Scramble in Write-ins," November 14, 1972; "Letter to the Editor: Helped Economy," May 7, 1973; "Dorothy Baker Dies Suddenly," May 14, 1973; "Letter to the Editor: Ida, Not Dorothy," January 16, 1974; September 29, 1974.

Jourdonnais, E. L. "Five Gallon Liquor Used for Party." *Choteau Acantha 1934. Microfilm.*

Lincoln, Marga. "Prohibition in Helena: When the Nation was 'Dry,' Liquor Still Flowed." *Independent Record* (Helena, MT). October 27, 2013; "Bluestone House's Past Shrouded in Mystery." *Independent Record* (Helena, MT). December 22, 2013.

Logan, Sean. "Fiery History: Several Fires in Helena's Early Years Helped Shape the Town." *Independent Record* (Helena, MT). January 19, 2014.

Luchter, Paul S. "Luck's Amazing Sports Lists." Online: www.luckyshow.org/ Amazing/amazingsportslists.bak.

Martin, Cy. *Whiskey and Wild Women: An Amusing Account of the Saloons and Bawds of the Old West.* Hart Publishing, New York, 1974.

McCrehin McKown, Lisa. *Find A Grave.* "Josephine 'Chicago Joe' Airey Hensley." January 19, 2012.

Melcher, Joan. *Montana's Watering Holes: The Big Sky's Best Bars.* Globe Pequot Press, Guilford, CT, 2009.

Merritt, Christopher William. "The Coming Man From Canton: Chinese Experience in Montana (1862-1943)." Dissertation, University of Montana, Missoula, May 2010.

"Montana Diary: Working Girls—Whorehouses and American Nostalgia." *The Economist.* February 29, 2008.

Montana Historical Society. "Biased Justice: Women in Prison." *Women's History Matters: Montana Suffrage 1914-2014.* Helena, 2014.

Montana Historical Society Officers and Members. *Contributions to the Historical Society of Montana with its Transactions, Act of Incorporation, Constitution, Ordinances, Vol. II.* State Publishing Company, Helena, 1896.

Montana Historical Society Staff. *Historic Helena: Women's Walking Tours.* Montana Historical Society Press, Helena, no date; *Not in Precious Metals Alone: A Manuscript History of Montana.* Montana Historical Society Press, Helena, 1976.

Montana Standard (Butte, MT). April 2, 1939; December 28, 1958.

Nash, Jay Robert. *Encyclopedia of Western Lawmen & Outlaws.* Rowman & Littlefield, Lanham, MD, 1989.

New North-West (Deer Lodge, MT). April 28, 1882.

New York Times (New York, NY). "Suit Against An Ex-Husband: Montana Woman Alleges She Lost Her Property Through A Trick," March 27, 1899; "Jury's Oddly Mixed Verdict: Both Parties to A Helena Suit Claim Victory by It," October 15, 1899.

Olsen, Kirstin. *Chronology of Women's History*. Greenwood Press, Westport, CT, 1994.

O'Neill, Peggy. "Bathed In Memories." *Independent Record* (Helena, MT). February 22, 2012.

Pawlyk, Oriana. "WWII 'Devil's Brigade' to Receive Medal." *Military Times*. Military Times Group & Gannett Government Media, Springfield, VA, 2015.

Petrik, Paula. "Capitalists with Rooms: Prostitution in Helena Montana, 1865-1900." *History of Women in the United States: Vol. 9, Prostitution*. Ed. Nancy F. Cott. Edwards Brothers, Ann Arbor, 1992.; *No Step Backward: Women and Family on the Rocky Mountain Mining Frontier, Helena, Montana 1865-1900*. Montana Historical Society Press, Helena, 1987.

Record-Herald. "Dillon Mines Are Described: Geological Survey Issues A Bulletin on Old Time Mining District." March 19, 1918.

Robison, Ken. *Montana Territory and the Civil War: A Frontier Forged on the Battlefield*. The History Press, Charleston, 2013; *Confederates in Montana Territory: In the Shadow of Price's Army*. The History Press, Charleston, 2014.

Rogers, Aurelia Spencer. *Life Sketches of Orson Spencer and Others: And History of Primary Work*. Geo. Q. Cannon & Sons Company, Salt Lake City, 1898.

Ropes, L. S. "Revival of Mining at Marysville, Montana." *Mining and Scientific Press*. Vol. 114. June 9, 1917. San Francisco, pp. 801-802.

Russell, Thaddeus. "How 19th Century Prostitutes Were Among the Freest, Wealthiest, Most Educated Women of Their Time." *A Renegade History of the United States*. Free Press/Simon & Schuster, New York, 2010.

Shors, Dave. "Dorothy's House Causing Headache." *Independent Record* (Helena, MT). September 26, 1972; "Probe Dorothy's Rooms, City Commissioner Urges." *Independent Record* (Helena, MT). October 3, 1972.

Skidmore, Bill. "Police Raid Closes Dorothy's Business." *Independent Record* (Helena, MT). April 17, 1973; "The Lock Stays on Dorothy's Door." *Independent Record* (Helena, MT). April 18, 1973.

Slaughter, William, and Michael Landon. *Trail of Hope: The Story of the Mormon Trail.* Deseret Book Company, Salt Lake City, 1997.

State v. Baker, 135 Montana 180 (Montana 1959). Supreme Court of Montana.

Sun River Sun (Sun River, MT). November 27, 1884.

Talwani, Sanjay. "Urban Renewal's Legacy: For Good or Ill, Helena Society, Commerce and Government Remain Forever Transformed." *Independent Record* (Helena, MT). February 20, 2012.

Tiede, Tom. "Big Dorothy Had Heart, But the Police Moved In," 1973. Helenahistory.org.

Times Herald (Olean, NY). April 3, 1925, p. 19.

Tollefson, Pamela Wilson. "Myron Brinig's Butte: Jews in the Wide Open Town." Dissertation, University of Montana ScholarWorks: Theses, Dissertations, Professional Papers. Missoula, 1994.

U.S. City Directories, Helena, Montana, 1892.

Chapter 3: Butte—A Corrupt and Wide Open Town

Anaconda Standard (Anaconda, MT). December 22, 1890; February 13, 21, 1891; "It Was a Big Haul: Lou Harpell Robbed of Her Jewels and Watch: A Burglar's Clever Work," August 7, 1893; "Bowed Down in Sorrow: Butte's Streets Filled with the Mournful Evidences of Her Great Grief: Burying the Heroic Dead To-Day," January 18, 1895; "An Important Arrest: Sheridan, Cohn and Williams Captured in Anaconda: The Evidence is Strong," August 13, 1898.

Associated Press. "Prostitution and Gambling 'Help Butte,' Says Mayor." *Billings Gazette* (Billings, MT). Evening Edition, October 18, 1968, pp. 1, 9; "Former Madam from Butte Dies," *Spokesman Review* (Spokane, WA). October 7, 1987, p. A10; "Ruby Garrett, Butte, Montana's Last Madam Dies at 94," *Huffington Post.* March 21, 2012.

Astle, John. *Only in Butte: Stories Off the Hill.* Holt Publishing Group, New York, 2004.

Baumler, Ellen. "Prostitution from Suite to Cellar in Butte, Montana." *Montana: The Magazine of Western History* (Autumn 1988), pp. 4-21; "The End of the Line: Butte, Anaconda and the Landscape of Prostitution." *Drumlummon Views* (Spring 2009), pp. 283-301.

Beaverhead County History Book Association. *The History of Beaverhead County Vol. 1 (1800-1920)*. Herff-Jones, Inc. Logan, UT, 1990, pp. 193-195.

Beverly Snodgrass Papers (1967-1968). Mss 341, Archives and Special Collections, Maureen and Mike Mansfield Library, University of Montana, Missoula.

Butte City Directory, 1890.

City and County of Butte-Silver Bow Montana. "Brief History of the Great Disaster of 1895." Co.silverbow.mt.us.

Chaplin, Charlie. *My Autobiography.* Simon & Schuster, New York, 1964.

The Chicago Directory Company. *Plan of Re-Numbering City of Chicago: Complete Table Showing New and Old Numbers Affected by an Ordinance Passed by the City Council of the City of Chicago.* The Chicago Directory Company, Chicago, 1909.

Chicago Tribune (Chicago, IL). "The Great Conflagration," October 11, 1871.

Daily Inter Mountain (Butte, MT). August 5, 1899.

Finnegan, Alice. *Goosetown in Their Own Words 1900-1945: An Oral History of Anaconda's Ethnic, Working-Class Neighborhood.* Sweetgrass Books, Helena, 2012.

Freeman, Harry Campbell. *A Brief History of Butte Montana: The World's Greatest Mining Camp.* Henry O. Shepard Co., Chicago, 1900.

Gevock, Nick. "Madam of Butte's Past—Ruby Garrett, Once Owner of Dumas Brothel, Dies at 94." *Montana Standard* (Butte, MT). March 20, 2012.

Grossman, Ron. "Even Sin Strips Have Redeeming Value—for Land." *Chicago Tribune* (Chicago, IL). May 26, 1985.

Hammond, Trevor. "The Great Chicago Fire: October 8-10, 1871." *Fishwrap: The Official Blog of Newspapers.com.* October 1, 2014.

Historical Encyclopedia of Illinois and History of Hancock County, Vol. II, Munsell Publishing, Chicago, 1921.

International Sex Worker Foundation for Art, Culture, and Education. NEW Enterprises. Ehrenberg, AZ, 2015.

Johnson, Curt, and Craig R. Sautter. *The Wicked City: Chicago from Kenna to Capone*. De Capo Press, Chicago, 1998.

Johnson, Charles S. "Saying Goodbye." *Missoulian* (Missoula, MT). March 13, 2005.

Keefe, Rose. *The Man Who Got Away: The Bugs Moran Story, A Biography*. Cumberland House Publishing, Nashville, 2005.

Kendall. "Hairtrigger Block." *The Chicago Crime Scenes Project: Photographs of Locations Associated with Infamous Criminal incidents in Chicago.* August 30, 2008; "Annie Stewart and Carrie Watson," August 30, 2008; "The Mansion," September 13, 2008; "South Wells St.," September 13, 2008; "Carrie Watson—Come In, Gentlemen," January 24, 2009.

Martin, Cy. "Judge May Call for Vice Probe." *Billings Gazette* (Billings, MT). Morning Edition, October 18, 1968, pp. 1, 2.

Miller, Ronald Dean. *Shady Ladies of the West*. Westernlore Press, Los Angeles, 1964.

Montana Historical Society Staff. *Not in Precious Metals Alone: A Manuscript History of Montana*. Montana Historical Society Press, Helena, 1976.

Montana Standard (Butte, MT). "James D. Freebourn Takes Bench in Butte District Court," January 5, 1965, p. 1; "Beverly Snodgrass Gets Loan, Takes Up Residence—in Butte," November 16, 1968, p. 8.

Montana Standard Post (Butte-Anaconda, MT). "Tony Delmoe Seeks $4000 from Beverly Snodgrass." March 17, 1965, p. 9.

Moynahan, J. M. *Butte's Red Light Humor*. Chickadee Publishing, Spokane, 2003.

Murphy, Mary. "The Private Lives of Public Women: Prostitution in Butte, Montana 1878-1917." *Frontier: A Journal of Women Studies, Vol. 7, No 3, Women on the Western Frontier* (1984), pp. 30-35. Also "Women on the Line: Prostitution in Butte, Montana 1878-1917." Master's thesis, Butte-Silver Bow Public Archives, Butte, AW MO57, 1983.

Tales of the Dumas Parlor House, Butte, Montana: The Mining City's Last Brothel, 1890-1992. Words & Ink, Butte, 1995.

Visit Ogden. "Ogden History: Ogden, Utah's Colorful History." Ogden Convention and Visitors Bureau, 2014. www.visitogden.com.

Weather Underground. Weather History for Butte, Montana, October, 1968.

Wiltz, Teresa. "The Chicago Fire." *Chicago Tribune* (Chicago, IL). December 18, 2007.

Wommack, Linda. *Our Ladies of the Tenderloin: Colorado's Legends in Lace.* Caxton Press, Caldwell, ID, 2005.

Workers of the Writers' Program of the Work Projects Administration in the State of Montana. *Copper Camp: Stories of the World's Greatest Mining Town Butte, Montana.* Montana State Department of Agriculture, Labor and Industry Books, Inc., New York, 1943.

Writers Project of Montana. *Copper Camp: The Lusty Story of Butte, Montana, the Richest Hill on Earth.* Riverbend Publishing, Helena, 2001.

Chapter 4: Great Falls—The Ladies of Rosebud Alley

Billings Gazette (Billings, MT). May 20, 1902.

Fergus County Democrat (Lewistown MT). "Justice Waddell Is Very Strict: Stanford Law Breakers Compelled to Dig Up Heavy Fines," August 13, 1907, p. 1; February 6, 1912, p. 1.

Great Falls Tribune (Great Falls, MT). October 7, 2013.

Havre Herald (Havre, MT). June 17, 1908, p. 4.

Herodes, Alisa. Unpublished Manuscript. Great Falls, 2010.

Inbody, Kristen. "Scarlet Stories." *Great Falls Tribune* (Great Falls, MT). My Montana section. October 6, 2013.

Moynahan, J. M. *Red Light Revelations: A Glance at Great Falls' Lusty Past 1889-1918.* Chickadee Publishing, Great Falls, 2007.

Swartout, Robert R., Jr. *Montana: A Cultural Medley.* Farcountry Press, Helena, 2015.

Wilson, Gary A. *Honky-tonk Town: Havre, Montana's Lawless Era.* Globe Pequot Press, Guilford, CT, 1976.

Wipf, Briana. "Upstairs Girls Leave Mark on State's Culture." *Great Falls Tribune* (Great Falls, MT). November 1, 2014.

Chapter 5: Missoula—Mary Gleim, the Flower of Garden City

Anaconda Standard (Anaconda, MT). "Missoula Matters," November 12, 1893; "In the District Court," August 22, 1894; "Mother Gleim's Sentence," September 15, 1894; "Mrs. Gleim," November 3, 1895; "Fresh Air: Mrs. Gleim is Once More A Free Woman," November 22, 1895; "Mother Gleim in Court: She Sizes Up the Jurors and Tells the Judge that None of Them Suit Her," February 18, 1896; "A Suit Begins," May 23, 1899; "County Records," May 24, 1899; "Ends the Case," October 25, 1899.

Baumler, Ellen. *Montana Moments Blog.* "Mary Gleim." May 23, 2012.

Baumler, Ellen, and J. M. Cooper. *Dark Spaces: Montana's Historic Penitentiary at Deer Lodge.* University of New Mexico Press, Albuquerque, 2008.

Briggeman, Kim. "The Madam of Missoula: 'Stories and Stones' Tour Resurrects Mary Gleim's Untold Story." *Missoulian* (Missoula, MT). October 26, 2008.

Butler, Anne M. *Gendered Justice in the American West: Women Prisoners in Men's Penitentiaries.* University of Illinois Press, Champaign, 1997.

Byorth, Susan. "History of Women Inmates: A Report for the Criminal Justice and Corrections Advisory Council," Montana Department of Corrections, Helena, 1989.

Cohen, Betsy. "Familiar Faces." *Missoulian* (Missoula, MT). May 6, 2007.

Daily Missoulian (Missoula, MT). April 13, 1912; April 10, 1913; January 24, 1914; February 23, 1914; April 8, 1914; June 14, 1914; September 5, 1914.

Dias, Meridith (editor). *Speaking Ill of the Dead: Jerks in Montana History.* 2nd ed., "Chapter 11, Missoula's Murderous Madam: The Life of Mary Gleim, 1888-1914." Globe Pequot, Guilford, CT, 2011.

Dolan, Rebecca Calabrese. "Dead Men Tell Their Tales." *Montana Kaimin.* University of Montana, Missoula, 2011.

Criminal Registers, England & Wales, 1791-1892 for John Edgar Gleim.

Helena Independent (Helena, MT). October 6, 1892; April 20, 1893; June 22, 1893; August 1, 1893.

Historical Museum at Fort Missoula. "Missoula History Minutes." Missoula, 2015.

Livingston Enterprise (Livingston, MT). June 21, 1890.

Maddox, Fletcher. *Reports of Cases Argued and Determined in the Supreme Court of the State of Montana: Embracing the October and December Terms, 1895 and A Portion of the March Term, 1896, Vol. XVII.* Bancroft-Whitney Co., San Francisco,1896.

Montana State Prison Convict Records. State Microfilm 36. Montana Historical Society Research Center, Helena.

New North-West (Deer Lodge, MT). February 14, 1896.

New York, Emigrant Savings Bank Records, 1850-1883. January 26, 1870.

Pacific Reporter, Volume 23. "McCormick V. Gleim et. al." December 4, 1893. West Publishing Company, Eagan, MN, 1894. pp. 1016-1017.

Ravalli Republican (Stevensville, MT). December 9, 1896.

Red Lodge Picket (Red Lodge, MT). September 22, 1894.

Ronan Pioneer (Ronan, MT). August 21, 1914.

Toole, John H. *The Baron, the Logger, the Miner, and Me.* Mountain Press, Missoula, 1984.

Western News (Stevensville, MT). December 19, 1900; March 6, 1901.

Chapter 6: The Madams of Miles City and Billings—Untamed Women on an Untamed River

Agnew, Jeremy. *Entertainment in the Old West: Theater, Music, Circuses, Medicine Shows, Prizefighting and Other Popular Amusements.* McFarland, Jefferson, NC, 2011.

Alice M. Edwards Family Narrative. June 9, 2012. Ancestry.com.

Anaconda Standard (Anaconda, MT). April 29, 1894; February 3, 1899; March 12, 1903.

Bancroft, Caroline. *Six Racy Madams of Colorado.* Big Earth Publishing, Boulder, CO, 1965.

Billings City Directory, 1901; also 1903, 1905, 1907, 1919, 1922, 1937. Ancestry.com.

Billings Gazette (Billings, MT). April 14, 1899; September 26, 1899; December 4, 1900; April 9 and 16, 1901; June 4, 7, and 21, 1901; June 10, 1902; July 18, 1902; August 8, 1902; September 9, 1902; October 21, 1902; April 3, 1903; August 21, 1903; September 29, 1905; August 20, 1907; February 5, 1909;

July 9, 1927; February 4, 1932; July 16, 1938; October 14, 1938; November 29, 1938; September 19, 1943; December 7, 1943 (Ollie Warren obituary).

Boise, Ada County, Idaho Marriage Certificate. Ancestry.com.

Bozeman Avant Courier (Bozeman, MT). February 28, 1873.

Broday, Linda. "Life on Soap Suds Row." *Petticoats & Pistols.* April 17, 2012.

Clawson, Roger, and Katherine A. Shandera. *Billings: The City and the People.* Billings Gazette/Montana Magazine. Billings, 1993.

Clarke, W. B. *Dusting Off the Old Ones.* Miles City, MT, 1961.

Cody Enterprise (Cody, WY). August 18, 1960.

Colorado Historical Markers: Waymark: House of Mirrors, Denver, April 20, 2008.

Colorado Statewide Marriage Index. Thomas M. Skerritt to Olive Dewey, page 10782. GS Film number 001690134. Digital Folder number: 005204202. Image Number: 03815. www.familysearch.org.

Conklin, Dave. *Montana History Weekends: 52 Adventures in History.* Globe Pequot, Guilford, CT, 2002.

Corbett & Ballenger's 19th Annual Denver City Directory, 1891. Denver Public Library Digital Collections.

Daily Intermountain (Butte, MT). September 6, 1900.

Daily Yellowstone Journal (Miles City, MT). November 14 and 18, 1882; May 15, 1885; January 7, 1886; February 6, 1886; July 13, 1887; December 4, 1887; August 7, 1888; December 11, 1892; March 22, 1894; April 28, 1894; May 12, 14, and 19, 1894.

Denver, Colorado City Directory, 1895, 1896, 1897, 1911. Ancestry.com.

Department of Agriculture, Labor, and Industry, State of Montana. *Federal Writers' Project: Montana: A State Guide Book.* Hastings House Publishers, Inc., Montana, 1949.

Erdoes, Richard. *Saloons of the Old West.* Gramercy Publishing, New York, 1997.

Fergus County Argus (Lewistown, MT). January 29, 1902; February 17, 1914.

Findagrave.com. John H. Samlin.

Great Falls Daily Tribune (Great Falls, MT). May 3, 1920.

Helena City Directory 1914.

Helena Independent (Helena, MT). March 16, 1893, morning, p. 5.

Hill, Rhonda. Transcribed. *Billings City Directory 1900-1901: A Complete Alphabetical List of Business Firms and Private Citizens, with Much Other Valuable and Miscellaneous Information.* Billings City Directory Co., Yellowstone County, Montana Genealogy and History.

Hoopes, M. D., and L. Lorman. *This Last West: Miles City, Montana Territory, and Environs, 1876-1886, The People, The Geography, The Incredible History.* Falcon Press Publishing, Helena, 1990.

Howard, Tom. "From the Editor: In Billings, History Sometimes Repeats Itself." *Billings Gazette* (Billings, MT). November 1, 2012.

Hull, Stephen. "Helena: The Shame of Montana," *Stag Magazine.* February 1953, pp. 17, 47.

Internet FAQ Archives. "Encyclopedia of Children and Childhood in History and Society: Th-W: Victory Girls."

Jiusto, Chere. "Tales Spun Along the Tracks: A History of Downtown Billings." Fall-Winter 1998. Yellowstone Historic Preservation Board, Billings.

Kemmick, Ed. "Records Reveal Miles City Survived Depression on 'Madam Money." *Billings Gazette* (Billings, MT). December 21, 2003.

KULR Channel 8 News: NBC. "Prostitution Trends." August 21, 2013.

Littleton Independent (Littleton, CO). "The Town of Sheridan: One of Denver's Beautiful and Flourishing Suburbs." November 9, 1894. Colorado Historic Newspapers Collection: Experience Colorado as It Happened.

MacKell, Jan. "Soiled Doves: An Overview of Good Girls Gone Bad in the American West." *True West Magazine.* September 30, 2013.

McLaird, James. "Calamity Jane: The Life and the Legend." South Dakota State Historical Society, 1994; *Calamity Jane: The Woman and the Legend.* University of Oklahoma Press, Norman, OK, 2005.

Merritt, Christopher William. "The Coming Man From Canton: Chinese Experience in Montana (1862-1943)." Dissertation; University of Montana. Missoula, Montana, May 2010.

Merritt, Dr. Chris, and Dr. Kelly Dixon. *Helena Daily Herald (1867-1878).* Collection of articles about Celestial Women.

Minneapolis, Minnesota City Directory, 1876.

Minnesota Death Index 1943. Record Number 936958, Olive Dewey McDaniels, December 5, 1943. State File Number/Certificate Number 023257.

Minnesota, North and South Dakota, and Montana Gazetteer and Business Directory, 1896, Vol. IX. R. L. Polk & Co., St. Paul, MN.

Montana County Marriages. January 23, 1903, Record 004351481; August 22, 1910; February 4, 1919, Record 004351449.

Montana History Wiki. *National Register of Historic Places Sign Text: Billings.*

Naugatuck Daily News. (Naugatuck, CT). October 26, 1897.

Olson, Eric. *Courting Justice: More Montana Courthouse Tales.* Dog Ear Publishing, Indianapolis, 2015.

Ostlind, Emilene. "The Bighorn Basin: Wyoming's Bony Back Pocket." *WyoHistory.org: A Project of the Wyoming State Historical Society.* Wyoming State Historical Society.

Pacific Reporter (Eagan, MN). Vol. 39. West Publishing Co., 1895.

Red Lodge Picket (Red Lodge, MT). April 6, 1900, p. 3.

River Press (Fort Benton, MT). May 3, 1882.

Rogers, Richard E. *Here Lies Colorado: Fascinating Figures in Colorado History.* Farcountry Press, Helena, 2005.

Sheridan, Wyoming, City Directory, 1910.

Thomas Skerritt. Ancestry.com.

Ulmer, Gregory L. *Heuretics: The Logic of Invention.* John Hopkins University Press, Baltimore, MD, 1994.

U.S. Federal Census. Arapaho County, Fort Logan, CO, District 0151. Thomas M. Skerritt; Middlesex, MA, Cambridge Ward 04, District 0717. Billings, Yellowstone County, MT, 1910, 1920, 1930. Walla Walla, WA, District 15. 1930. Harry E. Doherty; Littleton, Araphahoe County, CO. 1880. Olive Dewey.

Visit Ogden. "Ogden History: Ogden, Utah's Colorful History." Ogden Convention and Visitors Bureau, 2014. www.visitogden.com.

Wright, Kathryn. "Concrete With A Past." *Billings Gazette* (Billings, MT). October 22, 1972; "The Lucky Diamond: House Boasted Wealthy, Prominent Patrons." Billings Gazette (Billings, MT). June 20, 1982.

Chapter 7: Bozeman—A Hotbed of Vice

Bozeman Avant Courier (Bozeman, MT). May 15, 1879.

Bozeman Weekly Chronicle (Bozeman, MT). February 11, 1885.

Daily Yellowstone Journal (Miles City, MT). March 6, 1886.

Dillon Tribune (Dillon, MT). June 2, 1883.

Helena Weekly Herald (Helena, MT). January 15, 1874.

Livingston Enterprise (Livingston, MT). February 14, 1885.

Martin, Cy. *Whiskey and Wild Women: An Amusing Account of the Saloons and Bawds of the Old West.* Hart Publishing Co., New York, 1974.

Montana Wills and Probate Records, Gallatin County, Probate Case Files 1886-1894: Roberta M. Warn.

Nevada Tax Assessment List, 1865. Louise Couselle.

New York Wills and Probate Records, Kings County, Vol. 0232-0234, 1897.

Nicks, Charlie. *Big Medicine.* Xlibris, 2005.

Olson, Eric. *Courting Justice: More Montana Courthouse Tales.* Dog Ear Publishing, Indianapolis, 2015.

Schontzler, Gail. "Colorful Madams: Bozeman's Red Light District Thrived for 50 Years." *Bozeman Daily Chronicle* (Bozeman, MT). May 9, 2011.

Slate, Judy. "Bozeman Woman Uncovers City's Former Red Light District." *Kpax.com.* May 7, 2015.

Smith, Phyllis. *Bozeman and the Gallatin Valley: A History.* Globe Pequot, Guilford, CT, 1996.

U.S. Federal Census, 1880. Brooklyn, Kings County, NY; 1900. Billings, Yellowstone County, MT, District 0197.

Index

About the Author

Nann Parrett earned her BS in journalism at the University of Oregon and her MA in teaching at Concordia University, Portland. After working in publishing as a writer, editor, graphic designer, and web developer for over a decade in Idaho and Oregon, she switched careers to teach high school in Oregon. Since moving to Montana in 2009, she has been on the faculty at the University of Great Falls, where she teaches grammar, composition, writing for mass media, and writing for business. She is also the founder and executive director of Cultivate Helena, a nonprofit dedicated to promoting food equity through urban gardening projects that educate area youth about healthy local food and nutrition, composting, and sustainable gardening. She is married to author and professor, Dr. Aaron Parrett, and is the mother of a six-year-old girl, Maizy, who, like her mother, is interested in everything.